Green Marketing: A Comprehensive Guide

Authored By

Ibrahim Osman
Department of Marketing,
Tamale Technical University
Ghana

Mohammed Majeed
Department of Marketing,
Tamale Technical University
Ghana

Esther Asiedu
Department of Management Studies
Ghana Communication Technology University
Ghana

Jonas Yomboi
Department of Accounting
Valley View University
Ghana

&

Ebenezer Malcalm
Department of Management Studies
Ghana Communication Technology University
Ghana

Green Marketing: A Comprehensive Guide

Authors: Ibrahim Osman, Mohammed Majeed, Esther Asiedu, Jonas Yomboi & Ebenezer Malcalm

ISBN (Online): 979-8-89881-165-5

ISBN (Print): 979-8-89881-166-2

ISBN (Paperback): 979-8-89881-167-9

Published by Bentham Science Publishers Pte. Ltd. Singapore, in collaboration with Eureka Conferences, USA. All Rights Reserved.

First published in 2025.

need for a court order if at any point you breach any terms of this License Agreement. In no event will any delay or failure by Bentham Science Publishers in enforcing your compliance with this License Agreement constitute a waiver of any of its rights.

3. You acknowledge that you have read this License Agreement, and agree to be bound by its terms and conditions. To the extent that any other terms and conditions presented on any website of Bentham Science Publishers conflict with, or are inconsistent with, the terms and conditions set out in this License Agreement, you acknowledge that the terms and conditions set out in this License Agreement shall prevail.

Bentham Science Publishers Pte. Ltd.
No. 9 Raffles Place
Office No. 26-01
Singapore 048619
Singapore
Email: subscriptions@benthamscience.net

**BENTHAM
SCIENCE**

CONTENTS

FOREWORD

At a time when environmental concerns are at the forefront of global discourse, firms must rethink their marketing strategies to align with sustainability. *Green Marketing: A Comprehensive Guide* serves as a timely and insightful resource for scholars and businesses seeking to integrate sustainability into their marketing practices. This book digs into the fundamental principles and strategies of green marketing, offering a structured approach to understanding its relevance. It begins with an Introduction to Green Marketing, highlighting its evolution, importance, and impact on consumer behavior and corporate responsibility. To navigate the complexities of sustainable marketing, the book outlines the Key Rules of Green Marketing, emphasizing transparency, authenticity, and long-term commitment. It further explores Green Marketing Strategy, providing actionable insights into aligning environmental goals with business objectives.

A significant focus is placed on the Green Marketing Mix, where the traditional four Ps—Product, Price, Place, and Promotion—are reimagined through an eco-friendly lens. This discussion is complemented by an analysis of the Factors Determining the Adoption of Green Marketing, which examines the drivers and barriers businesses face when transitioning to sustainable practices. One of the most critical aspects of sustainable branding is Green Packaging, which has gained momentum as companies strive to reduce environmental impact. The book provides best practices and case studies illustrating innovative approaches to eco-friendly packaging solutions.

Finally, Green Marketing Communication is explored in depth, addressing the strategies brands can use to effectively engage consumers while avoiding pitfalls, such as greenwashing. The role of digital platforms, corporate social responsibility (CSR), and regulatory frameworks in shaping green messaging is also examined. As businesses and consumers become increasingly conscious of their environmental footprint, the need for genuine and effective green marketing has never been greater. This book serves as a practical guide, equipping readers with the knowledge and tools to implement sustainable marketing strategies that benefit both the planet and business performance.

I trust that this book will inspire and empower readers to embrace green marketing not just as a trend, but as a fundamental business philosophy that drives innovation, responsibility, and long-term success.

Dr Ahmed Tijani
Corporate Affairs & Information Technology (IT)
Minerals Commission
Ghana.

PREFACE

The global commercial environment has experienced a profound shift in recent times, primarily influenced by increased ecological consciousness and a growing emphasis on sustainable practices. With consumers becoming more environmentally aware, companies face mounting pressure to modify their approaches and incorporate sustainability as a fundamental principle. This transformation has led to the emergence of a crucial and dynamic concept: green marketing. This book, *Green Marketing: A Comprehensive Guide*, is designed to provide a thorough understanding of green marketing principles, strategies, and best practices. It is intended for marketing academicians, professionals, business leaders, and students who seek to integrate sustainability into their marketing efforts while maintaining a competitive edge.

The book begins with an introduction to green marketing, exploring its evolution, significance, and role in modern business. It then outlines the key rules of green marketing, offering guiding principles for companies striving to implement authentic and effective sustainable marketing strategies. A dedicated section on green marketing strategy provides insights into how businesses can align their sustainability goals with corporate objectives, ensuring that environmental efforts translate into brand equity and consumer trust. The discussion extends to the green marketing mix, where the traditional four Ps—Product, Price, Place, and Promotion—are examined from a sustainability perspective. The book explores factors determining the adoption of green marketing, including regulatory requirements, consumer demand, and competitive advantages. A special focus is placed on green packaging, as businesses increasingly look for eco-friendly alternatives to reduce waste and improve sustainability. This book offers guidance on crafting authentic, transparent, and persuasive messaging for companies while avoiding greenwashing—a practice that can erode consumer trust. In the current era of digital interconnectedness, green marketing has assumed new dimensions, with social media platforms and digital tools playing a crucial role in amplifying sustainability messages. As we embark on this exploration of green marketing, it is hoped that readers will gain valuable insights that will not only enhance their understanding of sustainability in marketing but also inspire meaningful change in their respective industries. The future of marketing is green, and through the lens of sustainability, businesses can pave the way towards a more responsible, ethical, and prosperous future. This publication serves as both a reflection of the current state of green marketing and a rallying cry for marketers worldwide to embrace sustainability as an integral component of their brand identity and business strategy.

Ibrahim Osman
Department of Marketing
Tamale Technical University, Tamale, Ghana

Mohammed Majeed
Department of Marketing
Tamale Technical University, Tamale, Ghana

Esther Asiedu
Department of Management Studies
Ghana Communication Technology University, Ghana

Jonas Yomboi
Department of Accounting
Valley View University, Ghana

Ebenezer Malcalm
Department of Management Studies
Ghana Communication Technology University, Ghana

CHAPTER 1

Navigating Green Marketing: Strategies, Benefits, and Challenges

Abstract: Green marketing (GM) can be viewed as a method of preserving both the environment and a means of ensuring a sustainable future across all sectors. The goal of this chapter is to lay the groundwork for green marketing within the context of this book. Green marketing, in general, helps firms achieve their environmental goals while also attracting and retaining customers, and encourages them to make more eco-friendly purchasing decisions. However, it faces several challenges, including high prices, a lack of standardization, and high operational costs. All stakeholders concerned (consumers, industrial purchasers, and suppliers) should be required to use GM. Additionally, to safeguard the planet from pollution and its effects, governments should implement stricter environmental regulations.

Keywords: Customers, Ecologically, Environment, Friendly, Green, Marketing.

INTRODUCTION

The 21st century has witnessed an escalating awareness of environmental issues, including climate change, biodiversity loss, pollution, and the depletion of non-renewable resources. These issues have prompted global discussions and actions toward achieving sustainable development goals (SDGs), as outlined by the United Nations. In response, both consumers and businesses are increasingly re-evaluating their roles and responsibilities in mitigating environmental degradation and promoting ecological balance (Kotler, Kartajaya, & Setiawan, 2017). In this context, green marketing, the process of developing and promoting products and services based on their environmental benefits, has gained significant traction in both academic discourse and managerial practice.

Green marketing is often considered a strategic and ethical response to mounting environmental concerns and shifting consumer values (Peattie & Crane, 2005). It seeks to address the demand for sustainability by emphasizing eco-friendly production, packaging, distribution, and post-consumption disposal. According to Polonsky (1994), green marketing goes beyond selling environmentally safe products; it encompasses a holistic approach to business operations that reduces environmental harm while providing economic and social value. As such, it serves

Ibrahim Osman, Mohammed Majeed, Esther Asiedu, Jonas Yomboi & Ebenezer Malcalm

as a key component of corporate social responsibility (CSR) and sustainability-oriented innovation (Chen, 2010).

The increased environmental consciousness among consumers has further accelerated the growth of green markets. Research indicates that consumers are more inclined to purchase products from companies perceived as environmentally responsible (Leonidou *et al.*, 2011). Nielsen (2020) study found that 73% of global consumers would definitely or probably change their consumption habits to reduce their environmental impact. This shift in consumer behavior has created market pressure on firms to adopt green marketing practices and visibly align their brand identities with environmental values (Delmas & Burbano, 2011).

Despite these positive trends, the integrity of green marketing has been questioned due to the prevalence of greenwashing, which involves the practice of conveying a false impression or providing misleading information about how a company's products are environmentally sound (Laufer, 2003). Companies engaging in greenwashing often capitalize on consumer environmental concerns without making substantial efforts to reduce their ecological footprint. This not only undermines consumer trust but also jeopardizes the legitimacy of truly sustainable businesses. TerraChoice (2010), in its "Sins of Greenwashing" report, found that over 95% of consumer products claiming to be green committed at least one form of greenwashing. Consequently, the rise of deceptive environmental marketing practices has led to a demand for greater transparency, third-party certification, and regulatory oversight.

Green marketing is not merely a promotional tactic; it is a comprehensive business philosophy rooted in the principles of sustainability, ethics, and stakeholder engagement (Ottman, Stafford, & Hartman, 2006). It requires a fundamental rethinking of product design, supply chain management, and consumer communication strategies. This chapter explores green marketing from both theoretical and practical perspectives, drawing on models, such as the Triple Bottom Line (Elkington, 1997), Stakeholder Theory (Freeman, 1984), and the Theory of Planned Behavior (Ajzen, 1991). It examines how businesses integrate green principles into strategic operations, the benefits and challenges associated with green marketing, and the evolving expectations of eco-conscious consumers. Special attention is given to the role of authenticity and innovation in building sustainable brand equity.

THEORETICAL FRAMEWORK

Understanding the foundations of green marketing requires a multidimensional approach that draws from established theories in business ethics, consumer behavior, and sustainability. The intersection of these disciplines provides both explanatory power and strategic direction for firms seeking to integrate environmental considerations into their marketing practices. This section presents three key theoretical frameworks that underpin green marketing: the Triple Bottom Line, Stakeholder Theory, and the Theory of Planned Behavior. Together, these frameworks provide insight into how businesses can align ecological responsibility with market performance and how consumer behavior is influenced by psychological and social factors within the context of sustainability.

Triple Bottom Line (Elkington, 1997)

The Triple Bottom Line (TBL) concept, introduced by John Elkington, shifts the performance evaluation of businesses beyond financial profit to include social equity and environmental sustainability. It proposes that companies should simultaneously focus on three key dimensions: *People (social equity), Planet (environmental protection), and Profit (economic viability)* (Elkington, 1997). In the context of green marketing, this framework encourages companies to develop strategies that do not merely aim for short-term gains but also prioritize long-term ecological and societal well-being.

Green marketing operationalizes the TBL framework by embedding environmental sustainability into product design, pricing strategies, supply chain management, and promotional campaigns. For example, using biodegradable packaging, reducing carbon emissions in logistics, and communicating authentic green credentials align with the "Planet" component, while fair labor practices and community engagement correspond with the "People" aspect. Ultimately, green marketing under the TBL paradigm seeks a holistic balance that ensures market competitiveness while addressing the urgent need for environmental stewardship and social responsibility (Savitz & Weber, 2006).

The TBL framework thus serves as a guiding philosophy for companies transitioning from traditional marketing to sustainability-oriented marketing. It helps align organizational mission statements, operational goals, and consumer expectations in a manner that contributes to global efforts toward sustainable development.

Stakeholder Theory

First proposed by R. Edward Freeman (1984), Stakeholder Theory emphasizes that the success of an organization depends on its ability to manage relationships with a wide array of stakeholders, not just shareholders. These stakeholders include customers, employees, suppliers, communities, regulators, environmental advocacy groups, and even future generations. In the realm of green marketing, this theory is crucial because sustainability-related decisions often have complex implications for multiple parties (Freeman, Harrison, & Wicks, 2007).

Green marketing responds to this pluralistic accountability by actively addressing the environmental concerns of diverse stakeholders. For instance, eco-labelling and transparency in green advertising cater to informed consumers, while compliance with environmental regulations ensures alignment with governmental expectations. Likewise, socially responsible practices, such as supporting local suppliers and community-based environmental programs, bolster stakeholder trust and loyalty.

Importantly, Stakeholder Theory shifts the motivation for green marketing from mere compliance or profit maximization to ethical obligation and relational sustainability. Firms are encouraged to engage in continuous dialogue with stakeholders, assess their environmental impacts from multiple perspectives, and co-create solutions that serve collective interests (Donaldson & Preston, 1995). In this way, green marketing becomes not just a set of tactical initiatives but a relational strategy rooted in ethics and mutual value creation.

Theory of Planned Behavior (Ajzen, 1991)

While TBL and Stakeholder Theory provide a macro and organizational perspective on green marketing, the Theory of Planned Behavior (TPB) offers a micro-level psychological framework to understand consumer decision-making in the context of environmentally responsible consumption. Proposed by Ajzen (1991), TPB posits that an individual's behavior is influenced by three key components: attitudes toward the behavior, subjective norms, and perceived behavioral control.

In green marketing, TPB helps explain why and how consumers choose to purchase eco-friendly products. A positive attitude toward sustainability, reinforced by societal norms (*e.g.*, peer pressure or media influence), and a belief that one has the ability to make a meaningful difference (behavioral control), all contribute to stronger green purchase intentions (Paul, Modi, & Patel, 2016). For example, consumers who believe that using reusable bags reduces pollution (attitude), observe their peers doing the same (subjective norm), and have easy access to such products (control) are more likely to adopt eco-friendly shopping behaviors.

Marketers use the TPB framework to design interventions that influence these determinants. Educational campaigns that shape favorable attitudes, social marketing that amplifies norms, and product accessibility that enhances control can jointly increase the adoption of sustainable consumer practices. Furthermore, TPB is instrumental in segmenting green consumers and tailoring messages to address specific behavioral barriers and motivations. In sum, TPB complements the broader frameworks of TBL and Stakeholder Theory by offering predictive insights into how consumers interact with green marketing messages and make environmentally conscious choices.

DEFINING CORE CONCEPTS

To grasp the practical and strategic implications of green marketing, it is essential to define its core concepts. These foundational terms serve as the pillars of environmentally responsible marketing strategies and reflect the dynamic interplay between corporate responsibility, consumer behavior, and environmental sustainability.

Green Marketing

Green marketing refers to the strategic process of planning, implementing, and controlling the development, pricing, promotion, and distribution of products in ways that minimize their ecological footprint (Peattie & Crane, 2005). Unlike traditional marketing, which often focuses solely on profit maximization, green marketing integrates sustainability into each component of the marketing mix. This includes using environmentally friendly raw materials, reducing energy consumption during production, and promoting products that are recyclable or biodegradable.

Importantly, green marketing is not only a reactive strategy to meet regulatory requirements or consumer pressure but also a proactive approach to creating shared value for businesses and society. It aims to align consumer demand with sustainability goals, thereby fostering both environmental stewardship and competitive advantage (Leonidou *et al.*, 2013).

Sustainable Branding

Sustainable branding involves the strategic alignment of a brand's identity, values, and practices with sustainability principles. It goes beyond simply offering green products to embodying environmental responsibility across the brand's touchpoints, including sourcing, messaging, and stakeholder engagement. According to Beverland and Farrell (2010), sustainable branding is characterized by transparency, authenticity, and a long-term commitment to creating ecological value.

Effective, sustainable brands build trust by clearly communicating their environmental efforts and being accountable for their environmental impact. This not only enhances brand equity but also attracts a growing segment of socially conscious consumers. Examples include Patagonia's commitment to circular fashion and Unilever's Sustainable Living Plan, both of which integrate environmental objectives into their core brand propositions.

Eco-Conscious Consumers

Eco-conscious consumers are individuals whose purchasing behavior is influenced by environmental considerations. Their consumption decisions are informed by a strong awareness of ecological issues, a sense of personal responsibility, and values that prioritize sustainability (Roberts, 1996). These consumers often evaluate products not just on price or quality but also on environmental impact, ethical sourcing, and corporate responsibility.

Research shows that eco-conscious consumers are more likely to support businesses that align with their environmental values and are willing to pay a premium for sustainable products (Nguyen *et al.*, 2020). However, their trust can be easily undermined by perceived inauthenticity or greenwashing, underscoring the importance of credible and consistent sustainability claims.

Greenwashing

Greenwashing is a deceptive marketing practice whereby companies exaggerate or fabricate their environmental credentials to appear more sustainable than they actually are. Delmas and Burbano (2011) defined greenwashing as the act of misleading consumers about the environmental practices of a company or the environmental benefits of a product or service.

Greenwashing can manifest through vague language (*e.g.*, "eco-friendly" without specifics), irrelevant claims, or false certifications. Although it may generate short-term gains, it ultimately damages brand reputation and erodes consumer trust. In today's era of social media and online transparency, consumers and watchdog organizations are increasingly vigilant, making it risky for companies to make unsupported sustainability claims.

STRATEGIC GREEN MARKETING APPROACHES

Companies aiming to authentically embrace green marketing must adopt a holistic strategy that incorporates environmental considerations into every stage of the marketing process. Below are four key strategic approaches commonly employed in green marketing.

Green Product Design

Green product design emphasizes the creation of goods that reduce environmental harm throughout their life cycles. This includes selecting sustainable materials, minimizing waste during production, ensuring product durability, and enhancing recyclability. For instance, Tesla incorporates renewable energy into its product offerings, such as electric vehicles and solar panels, exemplifying design innovation driven by sustainability (Hardman *et al.*, 2017).

Such practices not only reduce ecological impact but also appeal to environmentally conscious consumers who demand innovation aligned with environmental ethics.

Green Pricing

Green pricing strategies often reflect the added costs associated with sustainable sourcing, ethical labor practices, or environmentally safe technologies. This may result in premium pricing models. While some consumers are willing to pay extra for eco-friendly products, this approach can alienate price-sensitive segments (Gleim *et al.*, 2013). To balance this, companies must clearly communicate the added value of sustainability and offer tiered pricing where possible.

Innovative pricing approaches, such as carbon offset options or subscription-based models for reusable goods, can also make sustainable products more accessible and financially viable for a broader audience.

Green Promotion

Green promotion involves marketing communications that emphasize the environmental benefits of products or corporate sustainability efforts. Effective green promotional strategies use labels, certifications, and transparent messaging to validate environmental claims. Certifications, such as ENERGY STAR, Fair Trade, and USDA Organic, serve as credible third-party endorsements that enhance consumer trust (Chen & Chang, 2013).

Green advertising should be consistent and specific to avoid skepticism or backlash. Storytelling around environmental impact and corporate responsibility also fosters emotional connections with consumers.

Green Distribution

Green distribution aims to reduce the environmental impact of logistics and supply chain operations. Key practices include using electric or hybrid delivery vehicles, optimizing delivery routes, sourcing locally, and minimizing packaging waste. For example, IKEA has adopted flat-pack designs and local warehouses to reduce transportation emissions (Wiese *et al.*, 2012).

Additionally, reverse logistics—systems that allow customers to return used products for recycling or refurbishment—support circular economy principles and reinforce green brand positioning.

BENEFITS OF GREEN MARKETING

Green marketing is not merely a response to growing environmental concerns—it is also a strategic approach that offers tangible benefits for businesses in both the short and long term. By embedding sustainability into core marketing and operational strategies, firms can achieve economic, reputational, and regulatory gains. This section outlines the key advantages of adopting green marketing principles.

Competitive Advantage

One of the most compelling benefits of green marketing is its potential to deliver a competitive advantage. In markets characterized by intense competition and product saturation, environmentally responsible practices can serve as a powerful differentiator. Brands that commit to sustainable operations and transparently communicate their environmental efforts tend to stand out among consumers who are increasingly value-driven.

A notable example is Unilever, whose Sustainable Living Brands—those that integrate sustainability into their purpose and products—grew 69% faster than the rest of the company in 2019 and delivered 75% of the company's overall growth (Unilever, 2019). This performance underscores how sustainability can be harnessed as a value proposition that resonates with consumers, boosts brand equity, and enhances market positioning. According to Porter and Kramer (2011), companies that create shared value by addressing societal needs gain a long-term strategic edge.

Moreover, green innovation can open new markets and product categories. Companies, such as Tesla, Seventh Generation, and The Body Shop, have leveraged sustainability to redefine entire industries, thereby establishing leadership positions that are difficult for conventional competitors to replicate.

Consumer Loyalty

Consumer loyalty is another significant benefit derived from green marketing. Today's consumers are not only purchasing products—they are also investing in the values and ethics of the brands they support. Eco-conscious consumers, in particular, are more likely to remain loyal to companies that consistently demonstrate commitment to environmental sustainability (Nguyen *et al.*, 2020). Loyalty in this context is often linked to trust, which is built through transparent, authentic communication about sustainability initiatives.

Studies have shown that when consumers perceive a brand to be genuinely eco-friendly, their intention to repurchase increases, even if the product is priced higher than non-sustainable alternatives (Chen & Chang, 2013). Additionally, loyal green consumers often become brand advocates, sharing their positive experiences and influencing others through word-of-mouth and social media, which amplifies the brand's reputation and reach.

Long-term customer relationships built on sustainability also allow companies to better anticipate market shifts, co-create products with engaged audiences, and reduce the cost of customer acquisition through higher retention rates.

Cost Savings

Contrary to the misconception that sustainable practices are prohibitively expensive, green marketing can lead to significant cost savings over time. Environmentally responsible business models often incorporate resource efficiency, waste reduction, and energy conservation—each of which contributes to lower operational costs. For instance, companies that invest in energy-efficient technologies or optimize logistics to reduce fuel consumption can realize substantial savings.

According to the U.S. Environmental Protection Agency (EPA), organizations that adopt lean and green strategies typically reduce operating costs by 15–25% (EPA, 2020). Moreover, sustainable supply chain practices—such as sourcing local materials and using fewer packaging components—can streamline production and logistics, resulting in both economic and environmental benefits.

Cost savings also arise from the minimization of waste and the implementation of recycling or circular economy models. For example, firms like IKEA and Dell have developed take-back programs for used products, reducing raw material costs and enhancing environmental performance.

Regulatory Compliance

In an era of increasing environmental regulation, green marketing helps firms stay ahead of legal requirements, reducing the risk of fines, penalties, and reputational damage. Compliance with environmental laws—such as emissions standards, waste disposal rules, and product labeling requirements—is no longer optional but a necessary component of doing business, particularly in global markets.

By proactively adopting green practices, companies can avoid legal liabilities and demonstrate corporate responsibility. Regulatory bodies, such as the European Union (through REACH and the Ecodesign Directive) and the United States (*via* the EPA and FTC Green Guides), have established strict frameworks to ensure that environmental claims are truthful and verifiable. Firms that align their marketing with these standards not only mitigate legal risks but also enhance their credibility with stakeholders.

Additionally, regulatory compliance often opens access to government incentives, tax breaks, or green public procurement opportunities, particularly in countries where environmental policy is tightly linked to economic development (Testa *et al.*, 2012). This creates further financial and reputational incentives for companies to integrate sustainability into their marketing and operations.

CHALLENGES AND CRITICISMS

While green marketing offers multiple strategic and societal benefits, it is not without its challenges. Several criticisms have emerged around its implementation, effectiveness, and sincerity, raising questions about the extent to which green marketing can truly support sustainable development. This section discusses the key obstacles that firms encounter when adopting green marketing practices and the critical perspectives that have shaped the discourse.

Greenwashing

One of the most pervasive and damaging criticisms of green marketing is the practice of greenwashing. Greenwashing refers to the act of misleading consumers about the environmental practices of a company or the environmental benefits of a product or service (Delmas & Burbano, 2011). It often involves exaggerating sustainability claims, using ambiguous labels like "eco-friendly" without certification, or selectively disclosing only the positive aspects of a product's lifecycle.

A notorious example is the Volkswagen diesel emissions scandal. In 2015, the company admitted to installing software in diesel vehicles that manipulated emissions testing results, falsely presenting the cars as environmentally compliant. While marketed as "clean diesel," the vehicles actually emitted nitrogen oxide pollutants at levels up to 40 times above U.S. environmental standards (Hotten, 2015). This deception not only damaged Volkswagen's reputation but also highlighted how green marketing can backfire when misused.

Greenwashing undermines consumer atrust, weakens the credibility of genuinely sustainable brands, and distorts market competition. According to Lyon and Montgomery (2015), such deceptive practices may yield short-term gains but often result in long-term reputational and financial losses once they are exposed. Therefore, one of the core challenges for green marketers is maintaining transparency, traceability, and third-party verification in their sustainability claims.

Consumer Skepticism

Closely related to greenwashing is consumer skepticism, which has become a major barrier to the success of green marketing. As consumers are increasingly inundated with green messages, many struggle to differentiate between genuine efforts and marketing ploys. White *et al.*(2019) found that approximately 40% of consumers doubt the authenticity of green claims made by brands. This skepticism can reduce consumer engagement and hinder the effectiveness of even well-intentioned campaigns.

Several factors contribute to this distrust, including vague labeling, inconsistent certification standards, and previous experiences with greenwashing. Consumers may question whether a company's sustainability efforts are comprehensive or merely confined to a single product line. This "halo effect" leads to scrutiny not only of the specific product being marketed but also of the company's overall business practices.

To overcome skepticism, businesses must adopt clear communication strategies, use standardized eco-labels (such as Fair Trade, FSC, or ENERGY STAR), and engage in storytelling that illustrates real impacts. Empirical evidence suggests that consumers respond positively to messages that include verifiable data and third-party endorsements (Atkinson & Rosenthal, 2014). However, rebuilding lost trust remains a long-term process.

Cost Barriers

Another significant challenge is the high cost of sustainable production and green innovation. Transitioning to eco-friendly practices—such as sourcing organic materials, investing in energy-efficient technology, or achieving sustainability certifications—often requires substantial financial resources. These costs can be particularly burdensome for small and medium-sized enterprises (SMEs), which may lack the capital to compete with larger firms on sustainability fronts.

For instance, shifting to biodegradable packaging or renewable energy may offer long-term savings and reputational benefits, but comes with high initial outlays. In competitive markets, where price sensitivity is high, passing these costs onto consumers may reduce sales volumes. Moreover, when green products are priced at a premium, they often become inaccessible to low-income consumers, further limiting their market reach.

According to Peattie and Crane (2005), cost-related constraints not only affect supply chains but also pose strategic dilemmas. Should companies invest in costly green innovation and risk alienating price-sensitive segments? Or should they opt for minimal compliance, which may compromise their sustainability image? These decisions illustrate the complexity of integrating green principles into profit-driven business models.

To address this challenge, governments and industry associations can play a crucial role by providing subsidies, tax incentives, and green financing options. For example, the European Union's Green Deal includes funding programs to support businesses in transitioning to low-carbon operations. Such interventions help lower the entry barrier for sustainability and democratize access to green markets.

Market Segmentation Dilemma

The market segmentation dilemma in green marketing arises when companies struggle to align their sustainability values with the diverse socio-economic profiles of their target markets. While some consumers are willing to pay a premium for eco-friendly products, others may prioritize affordability over environmental impact. This divergence creates a tension between inclusivity and environmental idealism.

Green marketing strategies often appeal to affluent, educated, urban consumers who have the luxury to make ethical purchasing decisions (Leonidou *et al.*, 2011). However, this narrow focus risks excluding low-income consumers and reinforcing socio-economic inequalities. In developing countries or marginalized communities, where basic needs take precedence, green products may be perceived as elitist or impractical.

Moreover, cultural and regional differences affect how consumers perceive sustainability. A one-size-fits-all approach to green marketing may not resonate with diverse audiences. For example, in some regions, eco-conscious behavior is linked to religious or communal values rather than environmentalism per se, requiring marketers to localize their messaging and value propositions accordingly.

To address this challenge, marketers must develop tiered product lines, offering affordable green alternatives alongside premium versions. Brands like IKEA and Unilever have attempted to reconcile this divide by scaling sustainability in ways that balance price, accessibility, and impact. Inclusive green marketing must also involve education campaigns that raise environmental awareness across all demographic segments, not just the eco-elite.

CASE STUDIES

Case studies of leading companies offer tangible insights into how green marketing can be successfully implemented across different industries. These examples highlight the strategic integration of sustainability into business operations and brand identity, reinforcing consumer trust and delivering long-term value.

Patagonia – Sustainable Branding

Patagonia, a U.S.-based outdoor apparel brand, is widely celebrated for its unwavering commitment to environmental sustainability. The company's green marketing strategy is embedded in its core business model, particularly through its "Worn Wear" program, which encourages customers to repair, reuse, and recycle old gear instead of purchasing new items. This initiative not only reduces waste but also fosters a deeper emotional connection with the brand.

Patagonia's marketing campaigns consistently align with its environmental mission. For instance, their provocative "Don't Buy This Jacket" ad campaign urged consumers to think critically about consumption. While counterintuitive, this strategy enhanced the brand's credibility and resonated with eco-conscious consumers who value authenticity and transparency (Kleinhesselink, 2020).

Furthermore, Patagonia donates 1% of its sales to environmental causes and has even taken legal action to protect public lands, reinforcing its identity as an activist brand. These efforts exemplify how sustainability and branding can coalesce to create competitive differentiation and enduring customer loyalty.

IKEA – Green Operations

IKEA, the Swedish furniture giant, has made substantial progress in integrating green operations into its value chain. The company has pledged to become climate positive by 2030, aiming to reduce more greenhouse gas emissions than it emits across its entire value chain. This includes transitioning to renewable energy, minimizing waste, and promoting circularity. One of IKEA's most notable sustainability initiatives is its commitment to sourcing FSC-certified wood and cotton from sustainable sources. As of 2020, over 98% of the wood used in its products came from more sustainable sources (IKEA Sustainability Report, 2020). The company also offers services that encourage product reuse, such as furniture buy-back programs and recycled material initiatives. Green marketing at IKEA is not just an add-on but a strategic imperative, reflected in store designs, product development, and customer education. Through accessible pricing and mass-market appeal, IKEA has succeeded in making sustainable living more affordable and mainstream, addressing the market segmentation dilemma faced by many eco-brands.

The Body Shop – Ethical Sourcing

The Body Shop, a pioneer in ethical cosmetics, has built its brand around principles of fair trade, cruelty-free testing, and community sourcing. Since its founding, the company has emphasized transparency in sourcing raw materials and supporting the communities that produce them. The brand's Community Fair Trade program sources ingredients like shea butter from cooperatives in Ghana, ensuring fair wages and investment in local development. Moreover, its packaging strategies include refill stations, recycled materials, and initiatives aimed at reducing plastic waste.

The Body Shop's marketing emphasizes social justice, animal welfare, and environmental preservation, creating a multidimensional sustainability narrative. This approach resonates with consumers who prioritize ethical consumption, enhancing brand equity and loyalty (Sahota, 2014).

EMERGING TRENDS AND FUTURE DIRECTIONS

The landscape of green marketing is evolving rapidly, shaped by technological advancements, regulatory shifts, and changing consumer expectations. Several emerging trends signal a future in which sustainability is not only a moral imperative but also a source of innovation and competitive advantage.

AI and Blockchain for Green Supply Chains

Artificial Intelligence (AI) and blockchain technologies are revolutionizing green supply chain management by enhancing traceability, transparency, and efficiency. AI can optimize logistics to reduce emissions, predict sustainable sourcing options, and personalize eco-marketing content based on consumer behavior. Blockchain, on the other hand, offers immutable records that verify sustainability claims. For example, Everledger uses blockchain to track the origin of diamonds and other ethically sourced goods. Similarly, the textile industry is experimenting with blockchain to authenticate organic cotton and fair labor claims. These technologies address concerns of greenwashing and consumer skepticism by providing verifiable data and fostering trust. As companies seek to future-proof their operations, AI and blockchain will become integral to sustainable branding and accountability (Lim *et al.*, 2021).

Carbon Labeling

Carbon labeling is an emerging practice in which companies display the carbon footprint of their products on packaging or on their websites. This approach empowers consumers to make informed decisions and encourages firms to reduce emissions. Brands like Oatly and Quorn have adopted carbon labeling to highlight their lower environmental impact compared to traditional alternatives. Research shows that such transparency can influence consumer behavior, especially among eco-conscious millennials and Gen Z (Thøgersen & Nielsen, 2016). Carbon labels may soon become a regulatory requirement in some markets, pushing companies toward life cycle assessments (LCA) and carbon reduction strategies. Green marketing will increasingly involve not only communicating sustainability values but quantifying them with credible data.

Digital Green Campaigns

Social media platforms are increasingly used for environmental storytelling, allowing brands to reach and engage with diverse audiences. Digital green campaigns leverage influencers, short-form videos, and interactive content to promote sustainability narratives. For example, Lush Cosmetics uses Instagram and YouTube to showcase its packaging-free products and ethical practices, while also involving customers in advocacy initiatives. These campaigns often incorporate user-generated content, creating a sense of community and shared purpose. According to Lim *et al.*(2021), the effectiveness of digital green marketing depends on authenticity, interactivity, and emotional appeal. As attention spans shrink and digital saturation grows, brands must craft compelling sustainability stories that stand out and invite participation.

Net-Zero Commitments

A growing number of companies are setting net-zero carbon goals, aligning with global climate agreements like the Paris Accord. These commitments require systemic changes across operations, supply chains, and product design. Companies, such as Microsoft, Nestlé, and Unilever, have pledged to achieve net-zero emissions by mid-century or sooner. This shift is reshaping competitive strategy, as investors, regulators, and consumers increasingly prioritize carbon accountability. Net-zero ambitions influence green marketing by setting measurable benchmarks for progress and holding brands accountable through public disclosures. Firms that transparently report on their net-zero pathways are more likely to gain consumer trust and institutional support.

MANAGERIAL IMPLICATIONS

As green marketing evolves from a peripheral initiative to a central strategic function, business leaders must recognize its multifaceted implications for organizational success. The following managerial considerations are critical for maximizing the impact and credibility of sustainability-driven marketing efforts:

Authenticity Matters

In an age of heightened consumer awareness and digital transparency, authenticity in green marketing is paramount. Consumers are increasingly skeptical of environmental claims, particularly when there is a perceived gap between a brand's communication and its actions. The risk of greenwashing, wherein companies exaggerate or falsify their sustainability credentials, can result in significant reputational damage and consumer backlash (Delmas & Burbano, 2011). Managers must ensure that sustainability claims are substantiated through verifiable practices and data-driven evidence. This includes clear messaging, avoiding vague terminology (*e.g.*, "eco-friendly" without context), and backing up statements with third-party certifications, such as Fair Trade, USDA Organic, or Energy Star. Transparency builds trust, and trust is foundational to brand equity in the green economy. Organizations should institutionalize checks and balances through sustainability audits and compliance mechanisms to maintain authenticity over time.

Education is Key

Green marketing is most effective when it is accompanied by robust consumer education. Many consumers lack the technical knowledge to distinguish between genuine and superficial sustainability claims. Therefore, brands must play a proactive role in educating their audience on why and how their products are environmentally responsible. This involves simplifying complex information (such as lifecycle assessments or carbon footprints) into accessible narratives and interactive content. Educational campaigns can use storytelling, infographics, influencer partnerships, and workshops to demystify sustainability and empower consumers to make informed choices (Peattie & Crane, 2005). Informed consumers are not only more likely to purchase green products but also to advocate for them, amplifying brand reach through word-of-mouth and social sharing. Education thus becomes a long-term investment in consumer loyalty and advocacy.

Long-Term Strategy

Green marketing should not be a short-term promotional tactic but a long-term strategic orientation. This means embedding sustainability principles into the core business model, from product design and supply chain management to employee engagement and corporate governance.

According to Elkington's Triple Bottom Line framework (1997), firms must balance people, planet, and profit. Effective green marketing reflects this holistic approach, ensuring that environmental objectives are integrated into financial and social strategies. Companies like Interface, which have transformed their entire production system to become carbon negative, exemplify how the deep integration of sustainability leads to long-term resilience and differentiation. Senior leadership must drive this integration by aligning green marketing with corporate mission, vision, and culture. This also involves fostering cross-functional collaboration between marketing, operations, R&D, and sustainability departments.

Measure and Report

To build credibility and manage performance, firms must invest in measuring, reporting, and communicating their sustainability efforts using standardized tools and metrics. This includes Environmental, Social, and Governance (ESG) metrics, carbon footprint calculations, and Sustainable Development Goal (SDG) alignment. Reporting frameworks, such as the Global Reporting Initiative (GRI) or the Sustainability Accounting Standards Board (SASB), enable businesses to benchmark progress and identify areas for improvement. Regular public disclosure not only supports transparency but also attracts socially responsible investors and partners (Ioannou & Serafeim, 2015). Furthermore, the integration of third-party certifications reassures stakeholders that sustainability claims are externally validated, reducing the risk of credibility gaps and enhancing stakeholder trust.

CONCLUSION

Green marketing represents a transformative shift in how businesses engage with consumers, address environmental challenges, and pursue long-term competitiveness. It reflects the growing convergence of corporate responsibility and market differentiation, where sustainability is not merely an ethical imperative but also a strategic asset. This chapter explored green marketing from theoretical, practical, and critical perspectives. The Triple Bottom Line, Stakeholder Theory, and Theory of Planned Behavior provide robust frameworks to understand its foundations. Core concepts, such as eco-conscious consumers, sustainable branding, and greenwashing, shape the current discourse, while case studies of Patagonia, IKEA, and The Body Shop illustrate how these ideas manifest in real-world contexts. Despite its potential, green marketing is not without challenges. Consumer skepticism, high production costs, and segmentation dilemmas necessitate thoughtful strategy and continuous innovation. Emerging technologies like AI and blockchain, alongside practices, such as carbon labeling and digital campaigns, signal future directions that prioritize transparency, traceability, and engagement. Ultimately, the success of green marketing lies in its authentic integration into corporate DNA. Organizations must go beyond rhetoric, embracing sustainability as a long-term commitment that aligns actions with their values. By doing so, businesses not only meet the expectations of a rapidly evolving consumer base but also contribute meaningfully to global efforts in combating environmental degradation and fostering a more equitable, sustainable future.

REFERENCES

Akhil, A. (2017). Green marketing initiatives to meet consumer demands and sustainable development-challenges and opportunities. *SSRN,* 2980017.

[http://dx.doi.org/10.2139/ssrn.2980017]

Bhardwaj, A. (2021, April 22). A complete guide on green marketing, its importance & benefits. StartupTalky. https://startuptalky.com/green-marketing/.

https://brandshark.com/understand-what-is-green-marketing-and-its-6-key-elements/

Bhattacharjee, S., & Mukherjee, S. (2016). A descriptive study on green marketing trends in India. Environmental Communication: *A Journal of Nature and Culture*, 6(4), 441–458.

Delmas, M. A., & Burbano, V. C. (2011). The Drivers of Greenwashing. *California Management Review*, 54(1), 64-87.

Genç, R. (2017). The Importance of Communication in Sustainability & Sustainable Strategies. *Procedia Manuf., 8*, 511-516.
[http://dx.doi.org/10.1016/j.promfg.2017.02.065]

Katiyar, A., Katiyar, N. (2014). *A Conceptual Study on Challenges & Opportunity of Green Marketing in Developing Countries.*

Kotni, V. V. D. P. (2017). Problems & prospects of green marketing. MITS *International Journal of Business Research*, 4(2), 86–90.

Kotler, P., Kartajaya, H., & Setiawan, I. (2017). *Marketing 4.0: Moving from traditional to digital.* Hoboken, NJ: John Wiley & Sons. .

Leonidou, L. C., Leonidou, C. N., Palihawadana, D., & Hultman, M. (2011). Evaluating the green advertising practices of international firms: A trend analysis. *International Marketing Review*, 28(1), 6–33. .

Majeed, M. (2022). Green Marketing Communication and Consumer Response in Emerging Markets. In: Mogaji, E., Adeola, O., Adisa, I., Hinson, R.E., Mukonza, C., Kirgiz, A.C. (Eds). *Green Marketing in Emerging Economies*. Palgrave Studies of Marketing in Emerging Economies. (pp. 43–73). Palgrave Macmillan, Cham.
[http://dx.doi.org/10.1007/978-3-030-82572-0_3]

Maniatis, P. (2016). Investigating factors influencing consumer decision-making while choosing green products. *Journal of Cleaner Production, 132*, 215-228.
[http://dx.doi.org/10.1016/j.jclepro.2015.02.067]

Martin, D., Schouten, D.J. (2015). *Sustainable marketing. (1st ed.).* New Delhi: Pearson.

Osman, A., Othman, Y. H., Salahudin, S. N., & Abdullah, M. S. (2016). The awareness and implementation of green concepts in marketing mix: A case of Malaysia. *Procedia Economics and Finance*, 35, 428–433.

Peattie, K., & Crane, A. (2005). Green marketing: Legend, myth, farce or prophesy? Qualitative Market Research: *An International Journal*, 8(4), 357–370.

Uttman, J. (October 22, 2007). *Understanding the five key rules of green marketing.* https://thewisemarketer.com/ headlines/understanding-the-five-key-rules-of-green-marketing/

UKEssays (November 2018). Green Marketing In India: Importance and Challenges. Retrieved from https://www.ukessays.com/essays/management/green-marketing-in-india-management-essay.php?vref=1.

CHAPTER 2

Key Rules of Green Marketing

Abstract: In today's market, consumers increasingly expect corporations to act responsibly toward the environment and society, rather than focusing solely on profit. In response, businesses are adopting green marketing strategies to promote products that minimize environmental impact throughout their lifecycle. This chapter outlines the evolving principles of green marketing, emphasizing the importance of ecological sustainability, corporate social responsibility (CSR), transparency, and consumer engagement. It explains that effective green marketing requires companies not only to innovate eco-friendly products but also to communicate honestly and foster consumer empowerment. By integrating both environmental and social dimensions, green marketing can enhance brand reputation while encouraging sustainable consumption behaviors. This chapter also highlights the need for collaborative responsibility among companies, suppliers, and consumers to drive meaningful environmental change.

Keywords: Eco-friendly, Green, Marketing, Products, Rules.

INTRODUCTION

Green marketing has become a pivotal strategy for businesses responding to a global rise in environmental awareness and social responsibility among consumers. Defined broadly as the development and promotion of products based on their genuine or perceived environmental benefits (Fernando, 2020), green marketing integrates ecological considerations into all phases of product development, packaging, promotion, and disposal. Environmentally conscious consumers actively seek products that minimize harm to ecosystems, reduce pollution, and conserve nonrenewable resources.

Several factors contribute to this shift, including increased consumer awareness of environmental issues, corporate commitments to sustainability, and pressure from social and environmental advocacy groups (Ottman, 2008). The benefits of green marketing extend beyond environmental preservation—they also enhance public health and corporate reputation. However, the term "green marketing" carries nuanced meanings and is often conflated with related concepts, such as sustainable marketing and environmental branding. This chapter aims to clarify these distinctions and provide a theoretically grounded framework for understanding and applying green marketing principles.

As environmental concerns have intensified, companies worldwide have adapted their operations to incorporate sustainability, reflecting an emerging paradigm that links ecological stewardship with long-term business viability (Akhil, 2017). Yet, despite growing interest, green marketing remains an evolving field with ongoing debates about its efficacy and scope (Tiwari *et al.*, 2015). Therefore, this chapter presents the key rules and strategic considerations necessary for effective green marketing in the contemporary business landscape.

LITERATURE

Green Marketing (GM)

Green marketing, often used interchangeably with "environmental marketing" and "sustainable marketing," refers to business practices aimed at reducing environmental impact throughout a product's lifecycle (Majeed, 2022). However, it is important to distinguish these terms for clarity. While green marketing focuses primarily on environmental benefits, sustainable marketing encompasses broader social and economic dimensions, integrating the triple bottom line of people, planet, and profit. Environmental branding specifically relates to the messaging and identity that position a company or product as eco-friendly. Emerging research challenges traditional marketing paradigms by emphasizing strategies that reconcile commercial objectives with ecological and social realities (Peattie & Crane, 2005). Green marketing is thus not only about improving product design or advertising but about fundamentally rethinking the relationship between business, consumers, and the environment.

Theoretical Frameworks in Green Marketing The chapter draws on several theoretical perspectives to deepen the understanding of green marketing, which are as follows:

- **Stakeholder Theory** highlights how companies must balance the needs and expectations of diverse groups, including customers, suppliers, communities, and regulators, to achieve sustainability goals (Freeman, 1984).
- **Corporate Social Responsibility (CSR)** theory underpins green marketing by framing environmental initiatives as integral to ethical business practices and social performance (Carroll, 1999).
- **Consumer Behavior Theory** elucidates how environmental values, knowledge, and skepticism influence purchasing decisions (Laroche *et al.,* 2001; Delmas & Burbano, 2011).

These frameworks provide a critical lens to analyze both the opportunities and challenges in implementing green marketing strategies.

KEY PRINCIPLES AND CHALLENGES

Recent studies have emphasized several core principles of green marketing, such as transparency, eco-innovation, and consumer engagement (Chen, 2010; Peattie & Crane, 2005). Transparency is particularly critical given widespread consumer skepticism stemming from greenwashing, where companies exaggerate or falsify environmental claims (Delmas & Burbano, 2011). Accurate communication, supported by credible third-party certifications and detailed sustainability reports, can help build consumer trust.

Consumer engagement strategies that empower buyers to participate in sustainability efforts—such as through eco-labels or social campaigns—enhance the perceived value of green products (Ottman, 2011). However, research also identifies barriers, including limited consumer knowledge, higher costs, and mixed perceptions of product effectiveness (Joshi & Rahman, 2017).

RECENT ADVANCES IN GREEN MARKETING RESEARCH

To remain current, it is essential to integrate emerging themes, such as digital sustainability campaigns, ESG (Environmental, Social, Governance) reporting impacts, and the evolving dynamics of consumer skepticism (Leonidou *et al.*, 2021; Mohr *et al.*, 2020). Digital platforms now enable more transparent and interactive sustainability communications, while ESG metrics increasingly influence corporate strategy and investor decisions. Understanding these trends is vital for designing effective green marketing approaches that respond to contemporary challenges.

NEW RULES OF GREEN MARKETING

The new rules of green marketing reflect the evolving landscape of sustainability, consumer expectations, and corporate responsibility. The rules of GM are presented in Fig. (**1**). As businesses integrate environmental considerations into their strategies, the following principles guide effective and ethical green marketing:

Ecological Considerations

Ecological considerations should be central to advertising strategies. Businesses should use eco-friendly methods in their advertising, highlight the environmental benefits of their products or services, and clearly communicate their support for green causes to consumers. Green marketing encompasses everything from product design and packaging to pricing, promotion, consumer education, and social responsibility (Brandshark, 2023), aiming to attract new customers while also benefiting the environment.

Fig. (1). Principles of GM.

Eco-friendliness

The use of eco-friendly products and services with a low carbon footprint is a central aspect of green marketing. Appropriate and environmentally friendly resources must be used in their creation, and no damage must be done to the natural world during any stage of the product's life cycle for it to be considered "green" (Brandshark, 2023).

Social Responsibility

Corporate social responsibility refers to the extent to which a company takes steps during product development, marketing, packaging, innovation, and reuse to mitigate its impact on the environment (CSR Europe, 2017). When it comes to green marketing, it is not only about producing eco-friendly goods that matter; it is also about doing the right thing for the community. CSR, also known as "corporate conscience," "corporate citizenship," "social performance," "sustainable responsible business," or "responsible business," is an approach to corporate self-regulation. A company's CSR policy serves as an internal, self-regulating mechanism to monitor and ensure the firm's compliance with applicable laws, ethical standards, and global best practices. Corporate social responsibility (CSR) is an approach to doing business with the intention of making a good difference in the world for the benefit of the company's stakeholders, customers, employees, communities, and the general public. Beyond product-specific green initiatives, businesses that engage in "green marketing" (Brandshark, 2023) aim to improve both society and the environment in general. This includes helping underprivileged areas as well as taking steps to reduce the company's own trash. It requires thinking about environmental impacts alongside ethical and social factors. CSR studies have found that green management plays a crucial role in defining a company's identity at its core. One of the most important factors in a company's green image and green competitiveness is the extent to which it engages in environmentally responsible operations (Sellitto & Hermann, 2019). Green business practices have a significant impact on how customers perceive a company and their loyalty to it (Dutta *et al.,* 2008). Therefore, green marketing is grounded on corporate social responsibility's triple-bottom-line principle, which defines green marketing as the promotion of goods that are meant to be less harmful to the environment. The goal of social marketing is to increase the availability of high-quality goods that have fewer adverse environmental effects.

Transparency

The effectiveness of any green marketing campaign hinges on transparency and open communication. Companies must clearly disclose the environmental impact of their products and services while ensuring that any sustainability claims are substantiated. By doing so, businesses can demonstrate their commitment to eco-friendliness (Brandshark, 2023) and earn consumer trust. Customers need to believe in both the product and the claims made about it. However, consumers have become increasingly skeptical due to the widespread exaggerations that occurred during the early years of green marketing in the late 1980s and early 1990s. Therefore, it is vital to communicate a product's environmental benefits accurately and support them with credible evidence. To reinforce this commitment, companies should go beyond legal requirements by publishing detailed sustainability reports that include information about their suppliers and the origins of raw materials. This level of openness fosters greater consumer confidence in the brand and its offerings. Ultimately, honesty in business dealings builds trust, as those who are transparent have nothing to hide.

Customer Engagement

In order for a green marketing campaign to be successful, the marketer must engage the target audience. As soon as the consumer feels invested in the outcome, they will have a better grasp of the concept, and problems with pricing, etc., will be easier to handle.

Improve consumer agency

Businesses should make their customers feel empowered to make a difference, whether individually or as part of a community of users. One of the main reasons people choose environmentally friendly products is the sense of empowerment and positive impact associated with their purchase.

Innovation

Green advertising relies heavily on novel approaches. It motivates businesses to go outside the box in their quest to lessen their negative effects on the environment. Businesses are encouraged to be innovative in their pursuit of waste reduction, energy savings, and eco-friendliness in product design and development (Brandshark, 2023). Eco-innovation offers a range of new opportunities to boost revenue, depending on the technologies adopted, the alliances formed, and the strategies a company uses to inspire its customers (Uttman, 2007).

Sustainable Connections

If firms want to effectively communicate their ideas, products, or services, sustainable communication is the way to go. Sustainable marketing communication is defined by Martin and Schouten (2015) as *"messages and media directed to any of an organization's stakeholders for the purpose of achieving the organization's marketing and sustainability objectives."* A company's transparency, honesty, and accountability, as well as its capacity to develop its reputation and foster communities of intent, are all factors that should be considered when crafting truly sustainable marketing communications. Genc (2017) stated that effective communication between diverse internal and external stakeholders in sustainable development initiatives is crucial to encouraging sustainability and involving all relevant parties. Companies should integrate their current marketing messages with credible conservation-focused communication. By offering customers the opportunity to participate, they can help drive meaningful change. Including images of cultural objects can enrich the narrative and strengthen emotional connections. It is essential to demonstrate that green initiatives genuinely enhance the final product. To succeed, companies must also be willing to take risks and accept the possibility of public failure. Eco-friendly products should be positioned as equal in value to conventional alternatives, while environmental innovations should be paired with additional benefits, such as improved quality and durability.

Eco-pricing

Marketers may set a premium price for their "green" products due to the increased labor and material costs associated with producing them. As a result, the corporation should think about a more reasonable price and successfully target the right clients.

Placement of Customer Value

Firms can increase the mainstream appeal of conservation items by planning for them to perform as well as (or better than) alternatives, endorsing and distributing the consumer-wanted value of environmental products, and targeting relevant consumer market sectors.

Satisfaction of the Buyers

When a company's environmental initiatives are well-received by its customers, these customers are more likely to return for additional business (Trang *et al.*, 2019). Some businesses in today's cutthroat marketplace are making concerted attempts to improve the environment as a marketing strategy for retaining and attracting customers (Han *et al.*, 2019). As part of their brand loyalty strategies, companies are increasingly incorporating CSR (Han *et al.*, 2020). Customers are more likely to have a favourable impression of a company and its products if they believe the organization cares about the environment (Fonseca & Ferro, 2015). Providing the eco-friendly goods that consumers demand can boost the company's green reputation and win more customers in the process.

Advice for Consumers

Sustainability and green product education are also part of green marketing. It will be difficult to sell the items to clients if the sole selling point is that they are environmentally friendly. Thus, marketers should understand that they need to convince people by promoting the true quality and ethically demonstrating the product's performance. Therefore, the company should use eco-labelling schemes to help persuade consumers that their product is environmentally friendly.

"Approval" of "environmentally less harmful" products is given via eco-labeling schemes. Companies attempt to raise customers' awareness of the positive environmental impacts of their products by providing more information about those impacts and the products themselves, according to a review of the literature (Majeed, 2022). However, the precise nature of the connection between environmental consciousness and eco-conscious actions has yet to be determined. Tolliver-Nigro (2009) found that environmental consciousness does not lead to significant behavioral changes. The decision to buy and use a product can be influenced by the consumer's knowledge of the product's positive environmental impact (Murthy, 2010). Businesses employ methods, such as public service announcements and environmental product labeling, to help customers become more informed shoppers. Green marketing relies heavily on educating consumers so that they will prioritize environmentally friendly products over those with a greater negative impact (Brandshark, 2023). Crane and Desmond (2002) noted an increase in environmental consciousness among local consumers. Therefore, companies must prioritize environmental stewardship for the sake of their customers and the bottom line. Companies having a strong environmental track record are often viewed as progressive and well-run. According to Joshi and Rahman (2017), consumers' purchasing decisions are influenced by their limited familiarity with green products and related issues. One possible explanation for this is that people need more than a surface-level awareness of environmental and social issues to be motivated to change their purchasing habits. Consumers may be more likely to adopt greener consumption habits if they have a thorough understanding of the consequences of unethical consumption.

PRINCIPLES OF GM

Consumer-focused Marketing

Each business must prioritize its consumers and center its operations on what they need. The notion is that long-term, mutually beneficial connections can be built when the business adopts a customer-centric approach to marketing. Companies should focus on satisfying consumer needs rather than trying to create a market need for a product based on their offering (Bhasin, 2021). This shifts the emphasis from push to pull marketing and sales. It is crucial for businesses to consider the needs and perspectives of their customers. This will foster ongoing relationships with clients, as opposed to a transactional one. When companies prioritize their clients, their clients prioritize them (Business Jargons, 2022). According to this theory, a company can build a long-lasting and lucrative relationship with its customers by viewing marketing from the customers' point of view.

Customer Value Marketing

In line with this theory, businesses should not waste money on flashy marketing campaigns or rebranding without investing in ways to improve the quality of their products. Customers will appreciate them more if they increase the product's worth. Adding value to the firm and its offerings is the essence of customer value marketing. The organization should focus on providing genuine value to its customers rather than just delivering reduced rates and deals. Customers now have a greater variety and competition to choose from. Apple became a $1 trillion corporation because of its dedication to generating value for its customers (Bhasin, 2021).

Innovative/Inventive/Creative Marketing

The third tenet, inventive marketing, states that genuine product and marketing enhancements should be sought. Customers' tastes and preferences are constantly evolving, keeping pace with the rest of the world. Therefore, the company must continually seek better ways to safeguard against the potential loss of customers. As a result, the corporation must continually seek out cutting-edge innovations to retain its clientele. The business should strive to better meet the demands of its customers by developing new products and services. Sustainably effective marketing relies on constant refinement. New products must be inventive to attract customers. A business's responsibility is to create new items that customers will find desirable, long-lasting, and within their price range. The product itself need not necessarily be where innovation is introduced. Introducing a new taste or type to an existing product or creating a more affordable option are all examples of innovation (Bhasin, 2021).

Sense of Mission Marketing

The product itself is not as important as the company's larger social objective. This is because workers are more engaged and productive when they know they are contributing to a worthwhile cause and are part of a company with a clear mission (Business Jargons, 2023) that they can believe in. Instead of focusing solely on products, the corporation should describe its goal in broader social terms. This will also aid in providing better service to the staff. Customers get the impression that a company is serious about its business when its marketing efforts reflect it. It demonstrates that the business prioritizes both market success and community impact. Having this awareness is more valuable than increasing profits (Bhasin, 2021). The company's growth will be sustainable in the long run as a result of this.

Societal Marketing

According to this idea, businesses should prioritize customer needs alongside business goals and societal interests when making marketing decisions (Business Jargons, 2022). This sustainable marketing tenet emphasizes the triple bottom line of profit, satisfaction, and impact. The need for a company's visibility across demographics and as a go-to resource for problems rather than just another cash cow has elevated the significance of social marketing (Bhasin, 2021).

EMPIRICAL REVIEW

Green marketing has garnered considerable attention in both academic and business spheres due to the growing global awareness of environmental sustainability. Empirical research in this field has predominantly focused on consumer behavior, organizational strategies, and the impact of green practices on firm performance. The findings across various regions reveal important insights and variations in the adoption of green marketing.

A study by Peattie and Crane (2005) emphasized that green marketing has undergone three evolutionary phases: ecological marketing, environmental marketing, and sustainable marketing. These phases demonstrate a shift from a focus on pollution control to broader sustainable development goals. Their work suggests that firms are increasingly adopting a more integrated approach to environmental concerns, moving beyond compliance to value creation.

In emerging economies, green marketing is gaining traction, though with slower uptake. Rahbar and Wahid (2011), for example, examined Malaysian consumers and found that green product knowledge and environmental concern significantly influenced purchasing decisions. The study revealed that consumers who are more informed about environmental issues are more likely to buy eco-friendly products, even at premium prices.

Similarly, a study conducted by Chen (2010) in Taiwan found that green innovation has a positive influence on brand equity and competitive advantage. Companies that invested in green product development and effectively communicated environmental benefits were perceived as more credible and trustworthy, resulting in stronger customer loyalty. This aligns with stakeholder theory, which posits that ethical environmental behavior enhances a firm's legitimacy and performance.

In Africa, research on green marketing is still emerging. In Ghana, few empirical studies exist; however, available evidence suggests a growing consumer interest in sustainability. However, barriers, such as limited product availability, higher prices, and skepticism toward green claims, impede market expansion. Agyeman (2014) explored consumer awareness in Accra and found that while many consumers express environmental concern, their actions are constrained by affordability and accessibility issues.

Moreover, empirical research highlights the importance of transparency in communication. Yazdanifard and Mercy (2011) found that misleading green claims, or greenwashing, erode consumer trust and reduce the effectiveness of green marketing campaigns. This highlights the importance of verifiable claims and third-party certifications in fostering consumer confidence.

Overall, empirical studies suggest that green marketing is most effective when firms invest in genuine sustainability initiatives, communicate clearly, and understand the socio-economic contexts of their consumers. More research is needed in developing economies to guide context-specific strategies and policies.

GREEN MARKETING STRATEGIES

Green marketing strategies are organizational efforts to integrate environmental considerations into the marketing mix. These strategies aim not only to satisfy environmentally conscious consumers but also to contribute meaningfully to environmental sustainability. Successful green marketing strategies are comprehensive, covering product design, promotion, distribution, and post-consumption activities.

1. Green Product Innovation

Product innovation is a central component of green marketing. Firms are developing products that are biodegradable, energy-efficient, non-toxic, or made from recycled materials. For instance, Unilever has launched products with reduced water usage, while Tesla has revolutionized the automotive industry with electric vehicles. Such innovations reflect a proactive approach to sustainability and often serve as a firm's unique selling proposition.

2. Sustainable Packaging

Packaging plays a crucial role in shaping consumer perception and influencing environmental impact. Companies are increasingly adopting recyclable, compostable, or reusable packaging materials. Coca-Cola, for example, introduced its "PlantBottle," which is partially made from plant-based materials. Sustainable packaging not only reduces waste but also enhances brand image.

3. Eco-Labeling and Certification

Certifications, such as Energy Star, Fairtrade, and Forest Stewardship Council labels, provide consumers with reliable information about a product's environmental attributes. These labels build credibility and guide consumers in making informed choices. However, firms must ensure that claims are verifiable and comply with national or international standards to avoid accusations of greenwashing.

4. Green Advertising and Promotion

Green marketing messages must be transparent and backed by evidence. Effective green promotion highlights the environmental benefits of products without exaggeration. Firms like Patagonia are known for their honest and impactful green campaigns, including messages that encourage reduced consumption. Such authenticity enhances consumer trust and brand loyalty.

5. Cause-Related Marketing

Some companies partner with environmental organizations to support sustainability causes. This strategy not only reinforces the firm's green credentials but also engages consumers emotionally. For example, The Body Shop collaborates with wildlife preservation initiatives, aligning its brand with broader ecological values.

6. Sustainable Distribution

Green logistics involves optimizing supply chain processes to minimize carbon emissions, reduce energy usage, and minimize waste. Strategies include using electric delivery vehicles, optimizing transportation routes, and reducing packaging. Amazon, for instance, is investing in electric delivery fleets as part of its climate pledge.

To succeed, green marketing strategies must be authentic, comprehensive, and aligned with the firm's core values. Moreover, firms must conduct regular market research to understand evolving consumer expectations and adapt their strategies accordingly. In contexts like Ghana, affordability and accessibility should also be addressed to ensure wider adoption of green products and services.

MANAGERIAL IMPLICATIONS

The implementation of green marketing strategies presents both opportunities and challenges for managers seeking to align business goals with sustainability imperatives. Firstly, managers must recognize that green marketing goes beyond product innovation; it requires embedding environmental responsibility into the company's culture and operational processes. This holistic approach ensures that sustainability is not a peripheral marketing tactic but a core business value.

Transparency and authenticity are critical managerial concerns. Companies should avoid the pitfalls of greenwashing by investing in credible third-party certifications and providing clear, verifiable information about product life cycles and environmental impact. This transparency builds consumer trust and differentiates the brand in a crowded marketplace.

Additionally, managers need to cultivate consumer engagement by educating customers on the benefits and limitations of green products. Tailored communication campaigns that address common consumer concerns, such as price premiums or product efficacy, can increase acceptance and loyalty. Leveraging digital platforms and social media for interactive dialogue can also enhance this engagement, allowing consumers to participate actively in sustainability initiatives.

From a supply chain perspective, green marketing necessitates collaboration with suppliers to ensure that sustainability standards are met at every stage, from raw material sourcing to distribution. Developing partnerships focused on eco-innovation can lead to cost efficiencies and reduce environmental footprints.

Ultimately, measuring and reporting on sustainability outcomes are crucial for driving continuous improvement. Managers should adopt comprehensive ESG metrics to monitor performance and communicate progress to stakeholders. This accountability not only supports regulatory compliance but also enhances corporate reputation and long-term competitiveness.

CONCLUSION AND RECOMMENDATIONS

Green marketing represents a critical evolution in how companies approach their environmental and social responsibilities in an increasingly sustainability-conscious market. This chapter has demonstrated that effective green marketing requires a strategic, transparent, and consumer-centric approach that integrates environmental principles into all aspects of business operations.

The reviewed literature highlights that while green marketing offers significant opportunities for brand differentiation and building consumer trust, companies must navigate challenges, such as consumer skepticism, cost concerns, and risks of greenwashing. By applying theoretical insights from stakeholder theory, CSR, and consumer behavior, managers can develop more effective strategies that balance profitability with ecological stewardship.

Recommendations

The following are a few recommendations to develop effective green marketing strategies:

1. **Embed Sustainability Holistically:** Integrate green principles across product development, marketing, supply chain management, and corporate culture.
2. **Ensure Transparency and Credibility:** Use third-party certifications, transparent reporting, and honest communication to build consumer trust and combat greenwashing.
3. **Enhance Consumer Engagement:** Educate and involve consumers through tailored communication and digital platforms to foster sustainable consumption behavior.
4. **Collaborate Across the Value Chain:** Partner with suppliers and other stakeholders committed to sustainability to ensure consistent environmental standards.
5. **Monitor and Report Performance:** Adopt ESG metrics and sustainability reporting frameworks to measure impact and inform stakeholders.

Future research should explore the evolving role of digital technologies in green marketing and investigate consumer responses to emerging sustainability claims. Practitioners are encouraged to remain agile and responsive to shifting consumer values and evolving regulatory landscapes to maintain a competitive advantage in the green economy.

REFERENCES

Brandshark, (2023). Eco-conscious strategies: Unveiling the 6 key elements of green marketing. https://brandshark.com/understand- what-is-green-marketing-and-its-6-key-elements/

Bhasin, H. (2019). Green marketing – Definition, benefits, importance and examples https://www. marketing91.com/green-marketing- definition-benefitsexamples/

Bhasin, H. (2021). Sustainable marketing – Strategy, importance and principles https://www. marketing91.com/sustainable-marketing/

Business, Jargons (2023). Green marketing https://businessjargons.com/green-marketing.html

Crane, A., Desmond, J. (2002). Societal marketing and morality. *European Journal of Marketing, 36*(5/6), 548-569.

[http://dx.doi.org/10.1108/03090560210423014]

CSR Europe, (2017). About us http://www.csreurope.org/pages/en/about_us.html

Dutta, K., Umashankar, V., Choi, G., Parsa, H.G. (2008). A comparative study of consumers' green practice orientation in India and the United States: a study from the restaurant industry. *Journal of Foodservice Business Research, 11*(3), 269-285.
[http://dx.doi.org/10.1080/15378020802316570]

Fernando, J. (2020). Green marketing definition https://www.investopedia.com/terms/g/green-marketing.asp

Fonseca, L., Ferro, R. (2015). Influence of firms' environmental management and community involvement programs in their employees and in the community. *FME Transaction, 43*(4), 370-376.
[http://dx.doi.org/10.5937/fmet1504370F]

Han, H., Chua, B.L., Ariza-Montes, A., Untaru, E.N. (2020). Effect of environmental corporate social responsibility on green attitude and norm activation process for sustainable consumption: Airline *versus* restaurant. *Corporate Social Responsibility and Environmental Management, 27*(4), 1851-1864.
[http://dx.doi.org/10.1002/csr.1931]

Han, H., Yu, J., Kim, W. (2019). Environmental corporate social responsibility and the strategy to boost the airline's image and customer loyalty intentions. *Journal of Travel & Tourism Marketing, 36*(3), 371-383.
[http://dx.doi.org/10.1080/10548408.2018.1557580]

Trang, H.L.T., Lee, J.S., Han, H. (2019). How do green attributes elicit pro-environmental behaviors in guests? The case of green hotels in Vietnam. *Journal of Travel & Tourism Marketing, 36*(1), 14-28.
[http://dx.doi.org/10.1080/10548408.2018.1486782]

Joshi, Y., Rahman, Z. (2017). Factors Affecting Green Purchase Behavior and Future Research Directions. *International Strategic Management Review, 3*(1), 128-143.

Majeed, M. (2022). Green Marketing Communication and Consumer Response in Emerging Markets. In: Mogaji, E., Adeola, O., Adisa, I., Hinson, R.E., Mukonza, C., Kirgiz, A.C. (Eds.), *Green Marketing in Emerging Economies*. (pp. 43–73). Palgrave Macmillan, Cham.
[http://dx.doi.org/10.1007/978-3-030-82572-0_3]

Murthy, P. (2010). Strategic Green Marketing for Survival *SSRN,* 1650560.

Ottman, J. (2011). The New Rules of Green Marketing: Strategies, Tools, and Inspiration for Sustainable Branding (1st ed.). Routledge. .
[http://dx.doi.org/10.4324/9781351278683]

Ottman, J.A. (2008). The five simple rules of green marketing. *Design Management Review, 19*(4), 65-69.
[http://dx.doi.org/10.1111/j.1948-7169.2008.tb00143.x]

Sellitto, M.A., Hermann, F.F. (2019). Influence of green practices on organizational competitiveness: a study of the electrical and electronics industry. *Engineering Management Journal, 31*(2), 98-112.
[http://dx.doi.org/10.1080/10429247.2018.1522220]

Sachdev, S. (2018). Eco friendly products and consumer perception *International Journal of Multidisciplinary Research, 1*(5), 279-287.

Tolliver-Nigro, H., (2009), Green Market to Grow 267 Percent by 2015, *Matter Network.*

Uttman, J. (October 22, 2007). *Understanding the five key rules of green marketing.*https://thewisemarketer.com/headlines/understanding-the-five-key-rules-of-green-marketing/

CHAPTER 3

Green Marketing Strategy

Abstract: Green marketing is a phenomenon that has developed particular importance in the modern market. This concept has enabled re-marketing and packaging of existing products. Additionally, the development of green marketing has opened the door to opportunities for companies to co-brand their products into a separate line. The goal of this chapter is to map out green marketing strategies for practitioners. Green marketing is the practice of promoting products or services that are sustainable and eco-friendly. Companies that invest in green marketing benefit from increased customer loyalty and a positive brand reputation, while also helping protect the planet and contributing to a more sustainable future. However, this is just the tip of the iceberg. Therefore, the green market needs to take broader considerations into account before implementing concrete actions. The emergence of green products and their significance has begun raising awareness and supporting sustainable development, which is essential for future generations. Green marketing and green products not only protect the environment but also educate society on how to do the same.

Keywords: Eco-friendly, Environment, Green, Marketing, Strategy.

INTRODUCTION

Green marketing refers to the strategic process by which organizations develop, position, and promote products and services that possess environmental attributes or are produced through environmentally sustainable practices. As defined by Peattie and Crane (2005), green marketing encompasses a holistic approach that integrates environmental considerations into product design, raw material sourcing, production processes, distribution systems, and promotional strategies. This approach seeks not only to meet regulatory standards but also to appeal to a growing segment of environmentally conscious consumers. At its core, green marketing reflects an organizational shift toward sustainability, rooted in a comprehensive understanding of the interconnectedness between ecological preservation, business profitability, and social responsibility.

Underpinning the green marketing paradigm are key theoretical frameworks, such as the *Triple Bottom Line* (Elkington, 1997) and *Stakeholder Theory* (Freeman, 1984). The Triple Bottom Line broadens traditional notions of business success beyond financial metrics to include environmental stewardship and social equity,

Ibrahim Osman, Mohammed Majeed, Esther Asiedu, Jonas Yomboi & Ebenezer Malcalm

thereby reinforcing the multidimensional goals of green marketing. Stakeholder Theory further enhances this perspective by arguing that businesses have a duty not only to shareholders but also to a wide range of stakeholders, including consumers, policymakers, community members, and environmental advocacy groups. These theories provide a robust foundation for understanding why and how firms incorporate sustainability into their core strategies, encouraging them to adopt marketing practices that are not only profitable but also socially and ecologically sound.

Despite its growing relevance, the conceptual landscape of green marketing remains fragmented due to overlapping and sometimes contradictory terminology. Terms, such as "green marketing," "sustainable marketing," "eco-marketing," and "environmental branding," are often used interchangeably, leading to confusion about their scope and intended meanings. This chapter adopts a focused definition of green marketing as a deliberate and strategic organizational commitment to integrating environmental considerations into marketing functions in a manner that is consistent, long-term, and aligned with brand identity and consumer expectations. Unlike tactical efforts or short-term promotional campaigns, green marketing in this context involves a holistic transformation that affects every stage of the marketing value chain—aiming not just to signal eco-consciousness but to embed sustainability as a core brand ethos.

STRATEGY AND IMPLEMENTATION IN GREEN MARKETING

Effective green marketing is not merely a matter of promoting eco-friendly features; it requires a comprehensive and strategically embedded approach that transforms both internal processes and external engagements. A green marketing strategy encompasses both the internal commitment to sustainability, often referred to as organizational greening, as well as external initiatives, such as product eco-labeling, consumer education, and digital engagement. These strategies are crucial in aligning organizational objectives with the demands of a growing, environmentally aware consumer base and evolving regulatory landscapes. The implementation of green marketing strategies often spans multiple business functions, including supply chain management, research and development, product innovation, and communications.

Organizational Greening is the foundational step in strategic green marketing, wherein firms internalize environmental values and restructure their operations to minimize ecological footprints. This transformation is often championed by internal advocates or "green champions" who drive sustainability agendas within the company. The redesign of operations—ranging from sourcing to production—embodies this change. Interface Inc., a global flooring manufacturer, provides a leading example through its Mission Zero initiative, which aims to eliminate the company's negative environmental impact by 2020. Through innovations in manufacturing, recycling, and the use of bio-based materials, Interface achieved significant cost reductions while strengthening its brand equity as a sustainability leader. This example illustrates that operational greening, when aligned with strategic objectives, contributes not only to environmental preservation but also to long-term profitability and a competitive advantage.

Another critical dimension of green strategy is eco-innovation, which focuses on the development and application of new technologies and sustainable practices to create products that meet environmental standards while fulfilling consumer needs. Eco-innovation is often evident in sectors, such as automotive, electronics, and consumer goods. Tesla Inc., for instance, exemplifies this through its pioneering battery technologies and electric vehicles that significantly reduce emissions. Similarly, IKEA's commitment to using only sustainable wood and renewable energy throughout its operations reflects a deep integration of sustainability into product design and supply chain practices. Such innovations not only serve the environmental agenda but also signal brand differentiation, appealing to consumers who value progressive and responsible corporate behavior.

Eco-labeling and certification schemes represent another strategic tool in green marketing. These systems provide consumers with verifiable information about the environmental attributes of a product or service, enabling them to make informed decisions. Labels like the EU Ecolabel, Energy Star, and USDA Organic assure consumers of environmental compliance and performance, fostering trust and credibility. However, the proliferation of certification schemes, many of which lack uniform standards or third-party verification, can lead to consumer skepticism and confusion—a phenomenon known as "green fatigue." Thus, businesses must not only adopt credible labeling systems but also invest in consumer education to ensure the clarity and reliability of environmental claims.

In the digital age, digital sustainability campaigns have emerged as a powerful avenue for implementing green marketing. Social media platforms provide brands with the opportunity to engage directly with consumers, share compelling sustainability stories, and build communities centered on shared values. One of the most iconic examples is Patagonia's #DontBuyThisJacket campaign, which encouraged consumers to consider the environmental impact of overconsumption. This paradoxical message not only enhanced Patagonia's credibility as a sustainable brand but also sparked global conversations about responsible consumption. Such campaigns, when executed with authenticity and backed by genuine corporate actions, can significantly enhance brand loyalty and consumer trust.

In summary, an effective green marketing strategy requires a multi-pronged approach that integrates sustainability into core business operations while communicating value in clear, credible, and engaging ways. Organizations that lead in green marketing do so not only by offering environmentally friendly products but by rethinking their entire value proposition, from innovation and certification to digital storytelling.

CONSUMER BEHAVIOR AND SUSTAINABLE BRANDING

Understanding consumer behavior is critical to the successful implementation of green marketing. While organizations may adopt various sustainability initiatives, their market impact depends significantly on consumer reception and response. Behavioral science, particularly Ajzen's *Theory of Planned Behavior* (TPB), provides a robust framework for analyzing the motivations behind eco-friendly consumer choices. According to TPB, an individual's intention to perform a behavior, such as purchasing green products, is shaped by three key components: their attitudes toward the behavior, perceived social pressures (subjective norms), and their perceived control over the behavior (Ajzen, 1991). Green marketing strategies must therefore be attuned to shaping these behavioral antecedents in favor of sustainable consumption.

Eco-conscious consumers are a growing market segment characterized by heightened environmental awareness and a desire to reduce their ecological footprint through their purchasing decisions. These consumers are typically motivated by ethical values, concern for future generations, and a sense of responsibility toward the planet. Brands, such as The Body Shop and Seventh Generation, have built their identities around these values, using natural ingredients, ethical sourcing, and cruelty-free policies to differentiate themselves in the market. Their commitment to transparency and environmental integrity has helped cultivate a loyal consumer base that identifies with the brand beyond the functional attributes of the products. For these consumers, environmental responsibility is not just an added benefit—it is a prerequisite for brand loyalty.

However, the decision to purchase green products is often complicated by the issue of **green pricing and value perception**. Green products are often more expensive than their conventional counterparts due to the use of eco-friendly materials, adherence to ethical labor practices, and the implementation of sustainable technologies. This price premium can be a barrier to adoption, especially among price-sensitive consumers. To overcome this, marketers must effectively communicate the long-term value of green products through life-cycle cost analysis, durability, and health benefits. Tesla, for example, has succeeded in framing its electric vehicles not merely as environmentally superior but also as economically advantageous due to reduced fuel and maintenance costs over time. Similarly, companies offering biodegradable cleaning products emphasize safety for children and pets, positioning sustainability as a value-added proposition that transcends short-term cost considerations.

Consumer trust also hinges on the perceived authenticity and verifiability of environmental claims. Greenwashing—where companies exaggerate or fabricate environmental credentials—has made many consumers skeptical of sustainability narratives. To counteract this, successful green brands must ensure that their sustainability claims are supported by evidence, third-party certifications, and transparent reporting. They must also maintain consistency across touchpoints—from packaging and advertising to corporate social responsibility reports. The alignment between brand values and business practices is crucial for establishing credibility and trust, which in turn influences consumer behavior.

Furthermore, social influence and community engagement play a significant role in shaping sustainable consumption. Peer recommendations, online reviews, and influencer endorsements can amplify the appeal of green products. Brands that create platforms for user-generated content or sustainability challenges often see higher levels of consumer engagement. Campaigns that involve environmental activism or community-based sustainability projects can strengthen emotional connections between brands and consumers, thereby reinforcing positive purchase intentions.

BENEFITS OF GREEN MARKETING

The benefits of green marketing manifest across multiple levels—corporate, consumer, and societal. As sustainability becomes a defining factor in competitive advantage and stakeholder trust, firms are increasingly investing in green marketing not only to signal environmental responsibility but also to reap tangible economic and reputational gains.

At the corporate level, green marketing provides a strategic pathway to enhanced brand loyalty, regulatory compliance, and access to green capital. Organizations that embed sustainability into their brand identity tend to enjoy stronger consumer attachment, especially from environmentally conscious demographics. According to the Harvard Business Review (2022), firms with comprehensive ESG (Environmental, Social, and Governance) reporting are more likely to attract impact investors and gain favorable credit ratings. Furthermore, aligning business practices with environmental regulations helps firms avoid penalties and reputational risks while fostering constructive relationships with policymakers. For instance, Unilever's Sustainable Living Plan has not only improved the company's environmental footprint but also driven consistent financial performance and stakeholder trust. Similarly, firms that align with global frameworks, such as the UN Sustainable Development Goals (SDGs), are better positioned to access international markets and development funds.

From the consumer's perspective, green marketing enhances access to products that are safer, healthier, and ethically sourced. These benefits appeal particularly to consumers concerned with issues, such as chemical exposure, labor conditions, and environmental degradation. Products like fair-trade coffee, which ensures equitable pricing and ethical labor conditions for producers, or BPA-free plastics, which mitigate health risks from chemical leaching, are prime examples of how green marketing directly benefits end-users. These products often carry additional non-functional benefits, such as ethical reassurance and a sense of social contribution, which further strengthen consumer satisfaction and brand allegiance. Health-conscious consumers are particularly drawn to green products that emphasize wellness, transparency, and minimal environmental impact, creating niche markets that traditional branding often fails to capture.

On a societal level, the broader adoption of green marketing contributes to a reduction in environmental degradation and promotes public awareness of sustainability issues. As firms adopt greener practices in production and marketing, they help reduce the overall carbon footprint of consumer economies. These shifts are further amplified through public-private partnerships that promote sustainable development on a wider scale. For example, collaborations between corporations, NGOs, and municipal governments have led to large-scale initiatives in recycling, clean energy, and green urban development. Such efforts contribute to the normalization of sustainability in both business and civil society, encouraging behavioral change at the grassroots level. Additionally, corporate green marketing campaigns often serve as public education tools, reinforcing environmental values and influencing cultural norms around consumption and sustainability.

CHALLENGES AND CRITICISMS OF GREEN MARKETING

Despite its potential, green marketing faces significant challenges that can undermine its credibility and effectiveness. These include deceptive practices, consumer skepticism, and structural flaws in certification systems. For green marketing to be a truly transformative force, these issues must be critically examined and addressed through transparent governance, accountability, and stakeholder engagement.

One of the most serious criticisms is greenwashing, the practice of misleading consumers about the environmental benefits of a product or a company's practices. Greenwashing creates a false impression of environmental responsibility, eroding consumer trust and distorting competitive dynamics. The most infamous example is the Volkswagen emissions scandal, where the company falsely claimed its diesel engines met emissions standards while using software to cheat emissions tests. Similarly, H&M's Conscious Collection has been criticized for vague sustainability claims and a lack of transparency regarding supply chain practices. These examples highlight how greenwashing not only deceives consumers but also undermines the legitimacy of genuinely sustainable brands. The long-term consequences of greenwashing include consumer backlash, legal sanctions, and reputational damage that outweigh any short-term marketing gains.

Related to greenwashing is consumer skepticism, which arises from vague environmental claims, inconsistent messaging, and a lack of verifiable information. Research by Delmas and Burbano (2011) suggests that when consumers perceive green claims as insincere or unsubstantiated, their trust in the brand diminishes, resulting in reduced purchase intentions. This phenomenon is especially pronounced in saturated markets where multiple brands use similar environmental language without offering meaningful differentiation or proof. The overuse of generic terms like "eco-friendly," "natural," or "green," without third-party validation, contributes to a credibility gap that hampers the overall effectiveness of green marketing campaigns. Brands must, therefore, prioritize transparency and consistency, using clear metrics, third-party audits, and honest narratives to maintain consumer confidence.

A further challenge lies in the limitations of green certifications. While eco-labels and sustainability certifications offer a mechanism for standardizing and verifying green claims, they are often voluntary, fragmented, and lack global harmonization. The absence of uniform standards means that two products bearing the "green" label may vary significantly in actual environmental performance. Additionally, the proliferation of certification bodies—some credible, others less so—adds to consumer confusion. For instance, while certifications like the EU Ecolabel and LEED are widely respected, others may lack rigorous criteria or independence, undermining the credibility of certified products. Addressing this challenge requires stronger regulatory oversight, harmonization of certification standards across jurisdictions, and greater transparency in certification processes. Regulatory bodies must step in to ensure that green certifications are not merely marketing tools, but genuine instruments of environmental accountability.

CASE STUDIES OF SUCCESS AND FAILURE

The practical outcomes of green marketing strategies can be best understood through real-world case studies that demonstrate both success and failure. These examples offer valuable insights into what drives effectiveness and credibility in green branding—and what pitfalls to avoid.

A widely celebrated success story is that of Patagonia, a company that has successfully integrated environmental advocacy into its brand identity. Patagonia's initiatives—ranging from its Worn Wear program, which promotes product reuse, to its public support for environmental causes—have established the brand as a leader in sustainable business. The company's #DontBuyThisJacket campaign, which discouraged unnecessary consumption, was paradoxically effective in boosting brand loyalty and sales. Patagonia's commitment to activism, transparent supply chains, and corporate responsibility demonstrates that environmental stewardship can be a source of competitive advantage. The brand's ability to align its marketing messages with genuine operational practices is key to its credibility and market success. Its case exemplifies how a values-driven approach, when consistent and authentic, can create strong consumer relationships while advancing environmental goals.

In contrast, the case of BP's "Beyond Petroleum" campaign illustrates the risks of green marketing without substantive change. The campaign, launched in the early 2000s, sought to rebrand British Petroleum as a forward-thinking energy company committed to sustainability. However, the company's continued investment in fossil fuels, coupled with the 2010 Deepwater Horizon oil spill, rendered the campaign hollow and disingenuous in the eyes of the public. Critics labeled the effort as a textbook example of greenwashing—where branding was used to distract from environmentally destructive practices. The reputational damage suffered by BP in the aftermath serves as a cautionary tale for firms that prioritize image over integrity in their green marketing strategies.

Emerging economies are also demonstrating how green marketing can be tailored to local contexts with great success. Indian brands, such as Amul and Paper Boat, have integrated environmental and cultural values into their branding strategies to resonate with domestic consumers. Amul has adopted eco-friendly packaging innovations and sustainable dairy practices, while Paper Boat emphasizes traditional Indian beverages in biodegradable pouches, supporting both cultural preservation and environmental consciousness. These brands show that green marketing in emerging markets must be sensitive to local traditions, affordability concerns, and infrastructural realities. Their success lies in combining sustainability with cultural relevance and affordability—a blueprint that other emerging-market firms can emulate.

MANAGERIAL IMPLICATIONS AND BEST PRACTICES

The strategic implementation of green marketing demands not only visionary thinking but also grounded operational discipline. For managers, translating sustainability ideals into actionable business strategies requires a careful alignment of values, resources, and communication frameworks. The transition from conventional marketing to green marketing is not merely cosmetic—it must penetrate the structural, cultural, and procedural layers of the organization.

First and foremost, green marketing must align with the core brand identity and values. This alignment ensures consistency across messaging, corporate behavior, and consumer expectations. When green initiatives are perceived as authentic extensions of a brand's philosophy—as seen in the cases of Patagonia or The Body Shop—they enhance brand loyalty and consumer trust. However, if environmental claims appear incongruent with a company's broader operations, they risk being dismissed as opportunistic or deceptive. Therefore, managers must ensure that sustainability is not an add-on activity, but an intrinsic part of the company's DNA, embedded within its mission statements, brand storytelling, and strategic objectives.

A critical managerial priority is to avoid superficial or symbolic environmental claims. The temptation to capitalize on consumer environmental consciousness with minimal actual change—greenwashing—poses significant reputational risks. This calls for rigorous substantiation of claims through credible third-party audits and certifications. Recognized labels, such as Fairtrade, Forest Stewardship Council (FSC), and the EU Ecolabel, enhance legitimacy and reduce consumer skepticism. Furthermore, employee training is crucial for internalizing green practices at every level of the organization. A workforce that understands and believes in the company's environmental goals is more likely to deliver authentic consumer experiences and advocate for sustainability across functions.

Transparency plays a pivotal role in building and maintaining consumer trust. Managers must employ clear, consistent, and honest communication when conveying environmental initiatives to ensure transparency and credibility. Platforms, such as corporate sustainability reports, product labels, and digital storytelling (*e.g.*, via Instagram or company blogs), can be used to detail progress, challenges, and future goals. Moreover, adopting a proactive and long-term strategic orientation—rather than reactive marketing tactics—positions companies as genuine environmental stewards. This strategic posture not only aligns with growing regulatory expectations but also meets the demands of environmentally conscious investors, partners, and consumers.

FUTURE DIRECTIONS IN GREEN MARKETING RESEARCH AND INNOVATION

As global environmental concerns intensify and consumer expectations evolve, the field of green marketing must continuously adapt and innovate. Future research should address emerging technologies, sociocultural dynamics, and the evolving business landscape to strengthen the theoretical and practical relevance of green marketing.

A promising area is the integration of blockchain technology for supply chain transparency. Blockchain offers an immutable ledger system that allows firms to track and verify every stage of their product life cycle—from sourcing raw materials to final delivery. By enabling real-time, tamper-proof documentation, blockchain enhances consumer trust and regulatory compliance. For instance, food companies can utilize blockchain to track organic or fair-trade certifications, while apparel brands can document labor conditions and sustainable sourcing practices. Research can explore the adoption challenges, consumer perception, and regulatory implications of blockchain-enabled green marketing.

Another frontier lies in the use of artificial intelligence (AI) and machine learning to predict and influence green consumer behavior. AI can analyze large datasets to uncover patterns in eco-conscious purchasing, tailor marketing messages, and optimize product recommendations. For example, companies might use AI to forecast demand for biodegradable packaging or to design personalized sustainability campaigns based on customer behavior profiles. Scholars can investigate the ethical, strategic, and operational dimensions of AI-driven green marketing, particularly how to balance personalization with privacy and environmental goals.

Cross-cultural studies offer fertile ground for understanding how perceptions of eco-branding vary across regions and consumer groups. While Western consumers may prioritize reducing their carbon footprint, emerging market consumers might value affordability and social justice. This raises questions about how green marketing should be localized and adapted without compromising global sustainability standards. Comparative studies across geographies can inform multinational corporations on how to tailor their green messaging, product design, and pricing strategies to culturally specific needs.

The Return on Investment (ROI) of green marketing, particularly in emerging markets, is another critical area. Many businesses are still hesitant to fully commit to sustainability due to cost concerns. Quantitative research that demonstrates how green marketing enhances brand equity, customer retention, and long-term profitability could bridge this gap. Metrics, such as customer lifetime value, reduced churn, or operational savings from energy efficiency, could be used to build compelling business cases for green investments. Finally, practical product and packaging innovations deserve increased scholarly attention. Examples, such as biodegradable packaging made from seaweed polymers, mushroom-based insulation, or QR codes that link to a product's carbon offset history, highlight the convergence of sustainability and consumer engagement. Such technologies not only reduce environmental impact but also create interactive, transparent experiences that resonate with modern consumers. Future research could evaluate consumer responses to these innovations, assess their scalability, and explore the integration of these innovations into mainstream product lines.

CONCLUSION

Green marketing stands at the intersection of environmental responsibility, business strategy, and consumer engagement. As this chapter has demonstrated, it holds the potential to deliver not only ecological benefits but also competitive advantage, brand differentiation, and market leadership. However, for green marketing to be truly transformative, it must move beyond surface-level strategies and embed itself in the foundational practices and values of the organization. This chapter has highlighted that effective green marketing requires alignment with core brand values, credible practices validated by third-party standards, and transparent communication that fosters trust. It is not merely a communication tool, but a strategic framework that spans product development, operations, stakeholder engagement, and organizational culture. Companies that invest in building authentic, integrated green strategies are more likely to sustain consumer loyalty, navigate regulatory complexities, and secure investor confidence. Looking forward, green marketing must evolve through technological integration, cross-cultural adaptation, and rigorous impact measurement. The use of AI and blockchain, the exploration of culturally nuanced consumer behavior, and the assessment of financial returns from sustainability investments will shape the next generation of green marketing strategies. Additionally, innovation in eco-packaging and sustainable sourcing must be matched by a robust ethical framework that prioritizes both environmental integrity and consumer welfare.

REFERENCE

Bhasin, H. (2019). Green marketing – Definition, benefits, importance and examples https://www.marketing91.com/green-marketing- definition-benefitsexamples/.

Bhaskar, H.L. (2016). Green Marketing: A Tool for Sustainable Development. https://papers.ssrn. com/sol3/papers.cfm?abstract_id=2739324

Bhattacharjee, B., Mukherjee, S., Mukherjee, R., & Haldar, J. (2022). Easy fabrication of a polymeric transparent sheet to combat microbial infection. ACS Applied Bio Materials, 5(8), 3951-3959.

Corporate Sustainability Management. (2023). https://csmathsg.com/course-content/week-10/section--0-7-green-marketing-strategies/

Correia, E., Sousa, S., Viseu, C., Larguinho, M. (2023). Analysing the Influence of Green Marketing Communication in Consumers' Green Purchase Behaviour. *The International Journal of Environmental Research and Public Health, 20*(2), 1356.
[http://dx.doi.org/10.3390/ijerph20021356] [PMID: 36674112]

Emeritus, (2023). Is green marketing really good for business? If so, how? Jan 13;https://emeritus.org/blog/sales-and-marketing-importance-of-green-marketing/

Peattie, K., & Crane, A. (2005). Green marketing: legend, myth, farce or prophesy?. Qualitative market research: an international journal, 8(4), 357-370.

Polonsky, M. J. (2017). Green marketing. In: Charter, M., & Tischner, U. (Eds). *Sustainable solutions* pp. (282-301). Routledge.

Sharma, D.M. (2014). *Green Marketing and Its Implication in India.*https://papers.ssrn.com/sol3/papers.cfm?abstract_id=2520790
[http://dx.doi.org/10.2139/ssrn.2520790]

Tan, Z., Sadiq, B., Bashir, T., Mahmood, H., Rasool, Y. (2022). Investigating the Impact of Green Marketing Components on Purchase Intention: The Mediating Role of Brand Image and Brand Trust. *Sustainability (Basel), 14*(10), 5939.
[http://dx.doi.org/10.3390/su14105939]

Wandhe, P. (2018). https://papers.ssrn.com/sol3/papers.cfm?abstract_id=3298576

Zhang, G., Zhao, Z. (2012). Green Packaging Management of Logistics Enterprises. *Phys. Procedia, 24*, 900-905.
[http://dx.doi.org/10.1016/j.phpro.2012.02.135]

CHAPTER 4

Green Marketing Mix

Abstract: When it comes to promoting consumer rights, safeguarding the environment, and satisfying customer requirements, the green marketing concept encompasses a wide range of actions. Consumers today care more than ever before about the products they buy, and they also want those products to be kind to the environment. Green marketing protects customers from shady merchants and works to eliminate fraudulent practices, such as grey marketing and food adulteration. Green advertising is seen as a method for preserving the planet for generations to come. As more people become aware of the importance of taking care of our planet, a new market—the green market—has emerged, and with it, green marketing's potential to improve environmental security. Therefore, the purpose of this chapter is to elaborate on green marketing concepts.

Keywords: Distribution, Green, Marketing, Price, Product.

INTRODUCTION

Green advertising (GA) helps us save the planet for the next generation. It improves environmental security. A new business, known as the green market, has emerged in response to rising environmental awareness. Hotels need to implement comprehensive green practices to compete in today's market (Perera & Pushpanathan, 2015). The use of plastic and plastic-based products can be reduced with the use of green marketing. Since plastic does not decompose, it should not be used on Earth. One plastic item will remain on Earth indefinitely. Imagine how much trash would accumulate if everyone kept using plastic in the same way they do now. Instead of the natural beauty we witness now, we shall see forests and the oceans full of plastic (Bhasin, 2019). Green marketing encourages consumer interest in the purchase of ecologically responsible items (Groening *et al.,* 2018). The idea of GM is rising to prominence around the world. "Green" advertising, with its close ties to environmental protection, is increasingly seen as a powerful marketing strategy (Hasan & Ali, 2015) that can be applied to the promotion of a wide range of products, services, and ideas. A new business opportunity has opened up for the global economy as a result of the recent rise in environmentally conscious consumers. Since the 1980s, academics have shown an increasing interest in GM and other strategies for environmental

Ibrahim Osman, Mohammed Majeed, Esther Asiedu, Jonas Yomboi & Ebenezer Malcalm

protection. Green marketing and related ideas have gained traction since the early 1990s (Leonidou *et al.*, 2015). Understanding green purchase intention is crucial now more than ever before, due to developments in environmental, scientific, and networking technologies, such as the internet, and increased public awareness and concern regarding ecological challenges, including a growing population and global climate change (Cohe, 2014; Majeed *et al.*, 2022). Creating an environmentally friendly product, employing environmentally friendly packaging, implementing sustainable company processes, and concentrating marketing efforts on messaging that highlights the product's environmental benefits are all examples of green marketing. Green marketing, as defined by the American Marketing Association, is the promotion of goods widely believed to be harmless to the natural environment. As a result, green marketing encompasses a wide range of actions, including adjusting products, processes, and packaging, as well as revising advertising approaches. Companies employ green marketing to try to solve problems with costs or profits. Consumers, corporations, and governments all play critical roles in putting green marketing into action. However, its implementation is hampered by a number of factors, including a lack of consumer awareness, financial restrictions, a lack of robust scientific information, a dearth of stringent rules, and the pressures of competition. Creating and promoting goods and services that meet the demands of green-conscious clientele without sacrificing quality, performance, affordability, or convenience is what "green marketing" is all about. Hence, this chapter aims to discuss the green marketing mix of contemporary firms.

LITERATURE

Theoretical Foundations of Green Marketing

Green marketing, which refers to the promotion of environmentally friendly products and practices, is grounded in several theoretical frameworks that help explain consumer behavior and guide organizational strategies toward sustainability. Among the most influential theories underpinning green marketing are the Theory of Planned Behavior (TPB), Stakeholder Theory, and the Resource-Based View (RBV).

The **Theory of Planned Behavior (TPB)**, developed by Ajzen, posits that human behavior is driven by behavioral intentions, which are, in turn, shaped by attitudes toward the behavior, subjective norms, and perceived behavioral control. Within green marketing, TPB provides a lens to understand how consumers' attitudes toward the environment, the influence of societal norms (such as peer and media pressures), and their perceived ability to make eco-friendly choices impact their purchasing decisions. For instance, a consumer may intend to buy a sustainable product if they believe it benefits the environment (attitude), if their peers support green practices (subjective norms), and if they feel empowered to make such purchases (perceived control).

Stakeholder Theory extends the focus of business decisions beyond shareholders to encompass all relevant stakeholders, including customers, employees, communities, suppliers, and regulators. In the context of green marketing, this theory underscores the need for businesses to address the environmental concerns of various stakeholder groups. For example, a company that communicates its sustainability efforts transparently and engages its stakeholders in environmental initiatives can build trust, loyalty, and a positive brand image. Effective green marketing thus requires an inclusive strategy that acknowledges and responds to the expectations of all interested parties.

Ultimately, the Resource-Based View (RBV) of the firm emphasizes that a sustainable competitive advantage originates from the firm's unique internal resources and capabilities. When applied to green marketing, RBV suggests that an organization's commitment to sustainability—manifested in green technologies, sustainable supply chains, and eco-innovation—can serve as a distinctive competency. Such green initiatives not only enhance environmental performance but also offer a marketing edge by differentiating the company in a competitive market. Together, these theories offer a robust foundation for understanding and implementing green marketing strategies. They illustrate that successful green marketing is not merely about product promotion but involves aligning organizational values, stakeholder interests, and consumer behavior toward the broader goal of environmental sustainability.

GREEN MARKETING (GM)

A "green consumer" is someone who does not buy products that could potentially harm them or others in some way, such as through their manufacture, use, or disposal; their excessive consumption of energy; their generation of unnecessary waste; their reliance on materials from endangered species or ecosystems; their cruel treatment of animals; their negative impact on countries outside of their own; etc. Most people mistakenly believe that "green marketing" only applies to the advertising or promotion of products that have positive effects on the environment (Polonsky, 2017). Sustainability marketing and ecological marketing are two synonyms that mean essentially the same thing. Green marketing's primary objective is to advance a company's position in the market by increasing the product's visibility in the consumers' minds. All participants in the supply chain must have the same green marketing goals if this is to be achieved. Some of the most critical parts of a green marketing strategy are "market segmentation, green product creation, green positioning, green price determination, green logistics, sufficient residual management, green communication, green partnership development, and having an adjusted marketing mix" (Cui *et al.*, 2020). Consumers are becoming increasingly concerned about environmental issues on a global scale. This has led to the development of eco-friendly marketing strategies, which indicate rising demand for environmentally and socially responsible goods and services. It is challenging for businesses to provide their customers with eco- or green-friendly options, and even fewer businesses are able to do it all at once. Green business strength has been demonstrated across a wide variety of industries, and it deals with numerous environmental concerns.

GM MIX

Nguyen-Viet (2022) stated that green goods, green promotion, and green place make up the green marketing mix. Adapting the traditional marketing mix of pricing, product, promotion, and placement into a green marketing mix requires a thorough familiarity with the tastes and buying habits of today's consumers. Incorporating sustainability components into the marketing mix is what is meant by "greening" the mix. Marketing campaigns that emphasize eco-friendly products and services are known as "green marketing" (Polonsky, 2011). To satisfy and meet consumer needs and reduce negative impacts on the environment, and also invite consumers to care more about the environment, green marketing is a marketing mix planning process that utilizes changes in consumer awareness of products/services that are more environmentally friendly by changing products, making ways, and packaging more environmentally friendly. It follows that green marketing encompasses all forms of promotion (Source 1).

7 Ps of Green Marketing Mix

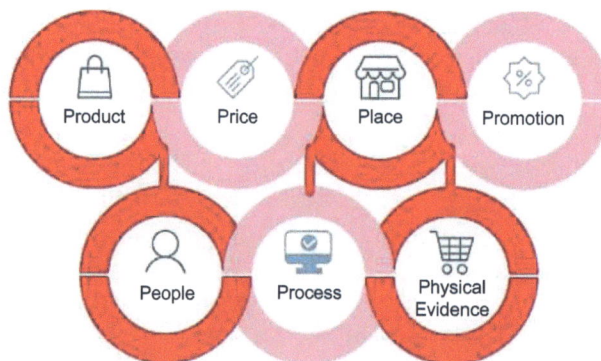

Product   Price   Place   Promotion

People   Process   Physical Evidence

Fig. (1). 7Ps of green marketing mix.

Green Product

Green products include both tangible items and service components. In addition to being eco-friendly, a "Green Product" is also safe to use. No product can be considered 100% eco-friendly. However, this category includes products that are energy efficient, environmentally friendly, and biodegradable. By enhancing and preserving people's quality of life without negatively impacting the natural world, Green Service embodies the principles of sustainable development.

According to Tseng and Hung (2013), consumers are more likely to purchase "green" products if they are environmentally friendly, reusable, recyclable, and made from all-natural ingredients. Kumar and Ghodeswar (2015) stated that "green" products are those made with safe materials and without harm to the environment. Reducing energy use, as well as heat and pollution emissions, is essential to achieving ecological development goals and ensuring the long-term viability of scarce resources. Products with a green label help the environment by reducing emissions and waste, using less energy, and using fewer or no harmful elements in their manufacture (Ottman *et al.*, 2006). There may be an opportunity to reduce the negative effects that products have on the environment once they are in use by applying five principles to their design. The 5Rs, as described by Peattie and Crane (2005), are "reuse, reconditioning, repair, remanufacture, and recycling." Businesses began producing and adopting green product policies as customers increasingly considered a product's hazardous content when making purchasing decisions. A green product is one that has been certified as such by a credible body and is made without the use of any harmful materials or processes (Kumar & Ghodeswar, 2015). If a company wants to have a greater impact on consumers than its rivals, it needs to produce ecologically friendly products. To do so, it must first determine the environmental concerns of its target market and then provide suitable solutions (Katiyar & Katiyar, 2014). Companies should produce environmentally friendly goods, as they reduce energy use and pollution. Protecting and conserving the environment at each stage of the production process for eco-friendly goods is a top priority. Environmentally friendly products utilize organic, non-GMO materials sourced from nearby farms and businesses, and their production and distribution have minimal or no adverse effects on the surrounding ecosystem. Products must be designed to meet the demands of consumers who value sustainability. Used or repurposed materials can be used to create a wide variety of products. Products that use less water, energy, and resources have fewer negative consequences on the planet. The development of products now increasingly centers on "green chemistry." For example, a marketer's role in product management may include relaying information about client demand for energy-efficient, organic, green-chemical, and locally sourced items to the product designer. Eco-labels, or certification labels indicating that a product is safe for the environment, have been a major topic of discussion. The question of whether this labeling should be done by the government or by an independent, private group is an important one. There is also the question of whether or not the entire country should be regulated by a single label.

The majority of shoppers are aware of the importance of eco-friendly goods. Consumers' awareness of the importance of selecting environmentally friendly items is crucial. According to the study's findings, the availability of environmentally friendly options is a major consideration for consumers when making purchases (Siddique & Hossain, 2018). Manufacturers must have items that are both durable and adaptable enough to be used outdoors in all types of weather and to protect their contents from rough handling by customers. Reduced packaging, smaller product sizes, and the use of biodegradable assets in place of non-renewable ones are just a few examples of how environmental products are expected to have less of an impact on the environment. Ecological goals in product development include minimizing waste and contamination while maximizing the efficient use of limited resources. Marketers play an integral part in product management by informing designers of market demands for environmentally friendly features, such as reduced energy consumption, organic ingredients, low chemical content, and regional production (Katiyar & Katiyar, 2014). There has been an undeniable increase in demand for eco-friendly goods, as consumers increasingly demand them. Businesses have begun investigating the green process, which includes creating corporate environmental profiles, monitoring and evaluating green performance, and boosting their public image. The need for green items has fueled greater rivalry among manufacturers to develop ever greener wares. Many nations already have eco-labeling systems in place to track and rate environmentally friendly products.

Green Price

A "green" pricing approach takes into account both the financial and ecological consequences of advertising. The value or worth of a product or service is reflected in the price that consumers are willing to pay (or accept in exchange) for it. Pricing has traditionally been a barrier to widespread adoption and expansion of the market for environmentally friendly goods and services. The higher cost of components used to make green products compared to their non-green equivalents is one reason for this. Organic food grown with natural fertilizers, for instance, may cost more than conventionally grown food. The costs of production and delivery may also increase. A larger price tag may result, for instance, from the transportation charges of a more expensive, but less polluting, renewable energy fuel source. Firms can use pricing activities strategically, for instance, by offering rebates for the return of recyclable packaging or charging extra for environmentally damaging items (Katiyar & Katiyar, 2014). The environmental benefits are not always the decisive element when comparing the value and quality of a product to those of a competitor, but they are always a welcome bonus. Customers are expected to pay a premium for green items due to their higher quality and reduced environmental impact. Green pricing protects the well-being of workers and communities, preserves the earth, and maximizes profits in a way that benefits all parties involved. The only way to get them to pay more for a product is to convince them that it is worth it. This benefit could take the shape of enhanced efficiency, functionality, aesthetics, or flavor. When comparing products of similar value and quality, the environmental benefit may prove to be the determining factor. The increased cost of many eco-friendly options means they are out of reach for some consumers. Eco-marketing communication should aim to justify this and convince the buyer that the product's higher price is justified (Lewandowska *et al.*, 2017).

Green Place

In order to reduce carbon emissions from transportation, "green place" focuses on efficient logistics management. In India, for instance, they can obtain a license to produce and sell locally imported mango juice. This prevents goods from having to be shipped from afar, cutting down on both shipping costs and, more crucially, the carbon emissions caused by trucks. Products that are environmentally friendly are often promoted heavily, yet few consumers will go out of their way to purchase them. This can be done through in-store marketing campaigns, including the use of eye-catching displays or repurposed materials to highlight environmental and other benefits. Where and when firms decide to sell its products will have a significant impact on the number of buyers a brand attract. Green distribution centers have no negative impact on the environment, as they distribute eco-friendly goods. Adding policies that mandate eco-friendly behavior from manufacturers and wholesalers is an example of "greening the place" in the marketing mix. For its printer ink cartridge recycling program, for instance, Hewlett-Packard has partnered with Staples. Companies can establish eco-unions with channel partners to reduce the environmental impact of their combined activities by, for example, rearranging logistics to be more environmentally efficient (*i.e.*, delivering fewer, but fuller, cargos). Local production can help businesses save money by reducing the amount of money and resources spent on transportation and distribution. The monetary and environmental benefits of this are clear. Internet sales are more cost-effective for companies than traditional retail outlets. Only a small percentage of consumers actively seek environmentally friendly options. Successfully launching a new green product requires positioning it such that it appeals to a wide audience rather than just the environmentally conscious. Thus, a green community's focus is on efficient logistics that lessen the environmental impact of travel.

Green Promotion

Advertising, public relations, sales promotions, direct marketing, and on-site events are all part of the green promotion mix. By employing eco-friendly methods of promotion and outreach, green businesses can enhance their reputation among their target audiences. The public must be educated about eco-friendly goods and encouraged to buy them. Therefore, corporations today invest significantly in marketing and PR for eco-friendly goods. Green marketing strategies are those that emphasize the eco-friendliness of a company's products or services. Advertisements, press releases, and product packaging all have the potential to include environmental claims and appeals. Promoting items in an environmentally responsible manner, such as by posting profiles on social networking sites for green marketing, is an example of green promotion. Smart green marketers will be able to bolster their credibility in the eyes of their target audience by employing environmentally friendly advertising and public relations methods. Promotion in green marketing, as defined by the authors (Kordshouli *et al.,* 2018), centered on the many conventions adopted by businesses to attract consumers' attention through packaging, promotional advertising, and other initiatives.

Green marketing should provide consumers with useful environmental information that is connected to the company's operations. Unless it is supplemented by other company endeavors, it is unlikely to be a useful strategic instrument. Therefore, a shift in the product, process, or corporate focus is required to promote some genuine environmental attribute of a product or organization. It is not necessary for these adjustments to be strategic. Tactical actions, such as appropriate environmental sponsorships or minor product improvements, can be communicated through environmental communication. It is important for the firm to be transparent about the intended outcomes of such endeavors. If consumers perceive these efforts as greenwashing, they may disregard the campaign altogether or even take punitive action against the company by boycotting their products or filing complaints with the relevant authorities.

Green Physical Evidence

The physical location where the service is provided, along with any associated physical components, is referred to as the service environment (Muala & Qurneh, 2012). This is crucial since customers often base their opinions on physical evidence when evaluating a company's performance. Similarly, clients' first impressions of the quality of the service they receive may be shaped by the surrounding environment. Customer happiness can be significantly impacted by the physical environment, which includes factors, such as atmosphere, service quality, seat convenience, background music, the physical layout of the service facility, and the appearance of the staff (Al Muala & Al Qurneh, 2012).

Green People

In the context of service delivery, "people" refers to the workers who create goods or provide services (Muala & Qurneh, 2012). Employee-customer interactions are an integral part of the service industry and may contribute to clients' overall satisfaction. As a means of differentiating between products, services, channels, and brands, employees are a crucial part of any customer-centric business. Employees' efforts to improve their own knowledge, communication, and abilities, as well as those of the company as a whole, can have a significant impact on the company's bottom line.

Green Process

The green process is an important part of the broader green marketing mix. As described by Nagata and Okuda (2005), this is "the ongoing effort to re-examine the process on a company's product manufacturing lines to reduce the environmental burden imposed by raw materials and energy usage in order to cut down on costs without sacrificing quality." After previously using chemical-based adhesives to attach acoustic foam to computer panels, IBM has switched to using dart-shaped connectors. This modification allowed IBM to lessen its production-related greenhouse gas emissions and made product recycling simpler at the end of its useful life (Kelly, 2008). Client happiness can be directly attributed to the transparency with which the process and the service providers' abilities are presented to the client. Maintaining a healthy balance between demand and supply of services in the face of process management's simultaneous consumption and production is no easy feat. Important steps in making and shipping a product include careful planning and execution. Sustainable procedures have a favorable effect on the product, according to research by Xie *et al.*(2019), which can boost a business's bottom line. The private sector has been paying increasing attention to green technology lately. According to Signh *et al.*(2018), traditional methods transform raw materials into finished goods that satisfy consumer demands. The goal of a sustainable process, on the other hand, is to maintain output while decreasing consumption and waste.

IMPLICATIONS

The research has important ramifications for both green customers and advertisers, and it provides compelling evidence for ushering in a new era of environmental consciousness. According to the results, green products and green promotional activities appear to influence customers' purchasing decisions. Therefore, it is essential for marketers to continue initiatives aimed at disseminating information about environmental sustainability. More green information needs to be made available; therefore, marketers need to create more displays, offer sampling, engage in commercialization, and facilitate distribution. Entrepreneurs who see opportunity in the growing green market will do one of two things: 1) Find a gap in the market and create a product to fill it; 2) Create environmentally friendly products that have a smaller footprint than the competition. Products should be packaged in a way that minimizes waste and is environmentally friendly. Businesses can utilize the eco-friendliness of their products as a marketing tool. Companies should use sustainable practices throughout the manufacturing and packaging of their goods. They should create goods that have minimal environmental impact both during use and after they have been retired from service. Products that are better for the environment typically cost more than their less eco-friendly counterparts. A manufacturer should provide ecological products that not only prevent further environmental damage but also repair any current damage. Such items may cost more than the average consumer is willing to pay. Additionally, eco-friendly packaging and efficient distribution are of paramount importance. It is simpler to sell as "green" goods that are produced locally and in season, like vegetables grown on nearby farms. Environmental credentials, such as the possession of a CP certificate or ISO 14000 certification, should be highlighted in any communications with the market. A company's public profile could benefit from publicity like this. A corporation should also promote the fact that it invests in environmental safeguards. Moreover, supporting nature through sponsorship is crucial. Finally, eco-friendly goods will likely need their own marketing push. Most shoppers will be able to afford green items if the pricing is standardized. In addition, better distribution of items according to consumer needs would be facilitated by a rise in the availability of green spaces providing wider coverage, which in turn would make it simpler to attract the target customers. Green promotion is ineffective unless it is created to reach customers in a way that changes their minds about whether or not to make environmentally friendly purchases.

CONCLUSION

Sustainability marketing should be examined through the lens of the marketing mix, which remains a powerful concept in marketing that effectively manages and distinguishes marketing from other corporate activities. Firm resources, market conditions, and customers' ever-evolving needs all factor into a business's decision on how to implement its sustainable marketing mix. Furthermore, some components of the sustainability marketing mix may be more or less crucial depending on the situation. Ultimately, when making decisions about the components of the sustainable marketing mix, it is essential to consider how these components interact with each other. Products should be manufactured in a manner that minimizes their environmental impact and human health risks by reducing or eliminating pollution and toxicity. Additionally, the product needs to minimize waste and help conserve valuable resources. Customers will only pay more for items that they perceive as superior in terms of design, performance, aesthetics, taste, or any other criterion, making price a crucial factor in green marketing. There are three types of "green" advertising: those that highlight the product's environmental benefits, those that advocate for a more eco-friendly lifestyle, and those that showcase the company's commitment to environmental protection. Marketers can significantly influence consumer behavior by selecting the most effective distribution channel for their products, tailored to where they will be sold. It is common knowledge that the manufacturing of any kind necessitates substantial amounts of both energy and trash. Therefore, the company may find success with an eco-friendly advertising campaign.

REFERENCES

Al Muala, A., Al Qurneh, M. (2012). Assessing the relationship between marketing mix and loyalty through tourist's satisfaction in Jordan curative tourism. *American Academic & Scholarly Research Journal, 4*(2), 1.

Bhasin, H. (2019). Green marketing – Definition, benefits, importance and examples. https://www.marketing91.com/green-marketing-definition-benefitsexamples/

Cohen, S. (2014). The growing level of environmental awareness *The Huffington Post.*

Cui, L., Guo, S., Zhang, H. (2020). Coordinating a Green Agri-Food Supply Chain with Revenue-Sharing Contracts Considering Retailers' Green Marketing Efforts. *Sustainability (Basel), 12*(4), 1289.https://www.businessmanagementideas.com/marketing/green-marketing/20101 [http://dx.doi.org/10.3390/su12041289]

Groening, C., Sarkis, J., Zhu, Q. (2018). Green marketing consumer-level theory review: A compendium of applied theories and further research directions. *Journal of Cleaner Production, 172*, 1848-1866. [http://dx.doi.org/10.1016/j.jclepro.2017.12.002]

Hasan, Z., Ali, N.A. (2015). The Impact of Green Marketing Strategy on the Firm's Performance in Malaysia. *Procedia Soc. Behav. Sci., 172*, 463-470. [http://dx.doi.org/10.1016/j.sbspro.2015.01.382]

Katiyar, A., Katiyar, N. (2014). A conceptual study on challenges & opportunity of green marketing in developing countries *International Journal of Management and Commerce Innovations, 2*(1), 218-225.

Kumar, P., Ghodeswar, B.M. (2015). Factors affecting consumers' green product purchase decisions. *Marketing Intelligence & Planning, 33*(3), 330-347. [http://dx.doi.org/10.1108/MIP-03-2014-0068]

Kordshoul, H.R., Ebrahimi, A., Allahyari Bouzanjani, A. (2018). An analysis of the green response of consumers to the environmentally friendly behavior of corporations. *Iranian Journal of Management Studies,*

8(3), m315-m334.

Lewandowska, A., Witczak, J., Kurczewski, P. (2017). Green marketing today – a mix of trust, consumer participation and life cycle thinking. *Management, 21*(2), 28-48.
[http://dx.doi.org/10.1515/manment-2017-0003]

Leonidou, L.C., Fotiadis, T.A., Christodoulides, P., Spyropoulou, S., Katsikeas, C.S. (2015). Environmentally friendly export business strategy: Its determinants and effects on competitive advantage and performance. *Int. Bus. Rev., 24*(5), 798-811.
[http://dx.doi.org/10.1016/j.ibusrev.2015.02.001]

Majeed, M.U., Aslam, S., Murtaza, S.A., Attila, S., Molnár, E. (2022). Green Marketing Approaches and Their Impact on Green Purchase Intentions: Mediating Role of Green Brand Image and Consumer Beliefs towards the Environment. *Sustainability (Basel), 14*(18), 11703.
[http://dx.doi.org/10.3390/su141811703]

Majeed, M. (2022). Green Marketing Communication and Consumer Response in Emerging Markets.*Green Marketing in Emerging Economies.*. Cham: Palgrave Studies of Marketing in Emerging Economies. Palgrave Macmillan.
[http://dx.doi.org/10.1007/978-3-030-82572-0_3]

Perera, H. L. N., & Pushpanathan, A. (2015). Green marketing practices and customer satisfaction: A study of hotels industry in Wennappuwa divisional secretariat. Tourism, Leisure and Global Change, 2, TOC-13.
https://www.academia.edu/29448615/Green_Marketing_Practices_and_Customer_Satisfaction_A_Study_of_Hotels_Industry_in_Wennappuwa_Divisional_Secretariat.

Ottman, J.A., Stafford, E.R., Hartman, C.L. (2006). Avoiding Green Marketing Myopia: Ways to Improve Consumer Appeal for Environmentally Preferable Products. *Environment, 48*(5), 22-36.
[http://dx.doi.org/10.3200/ENVT.48.5.22-36]

Polonsky, M.J. (1994). A stakeholder theory approach to designing environmental marketing strategy Unpublished working paper

Siddique, M.Z.R., Hossain, A. (2018). Sources of Consumers Awareness toward Green Products and Its Impact on Purchasing Decision in Bangladesh. *Journal of Sustainable Development, 11*(3), 9-22.
[http://dx.doi.org/10.5539/jsd.v11n3p9]

CHAPTER 5

Factors Determining the Adoption of Green Marketing

Abstract: Green marketing is an emerging practice with the overarching goal of reducing environmental impact across the product life cycle. Internal and external factors significantly contribute to the implementation of green marketing in any business. Therefore, the purpose of this chapter is to identify and clarify the key elements that hinder the spread of green marketing. The internal and external elements that influence the adoption of green marketing are identified and classified following a thorough literature review. External influences include stakeholder pressure, competition, consumer behavior, business social responsibility, government and legislation, among others. Internal factors, on the other hand, encompass price, owner-manager attitude, and top-management perception and action. The findings of this chapter will help people learn that green products are not only beneficial for health but also for the environment, and that a healthy, sustainable ecosystem is essential to human life.

Keywords: External, Factors, Green, Marketing, Internal.

INTRODUCTION

Managers are under pressure from the global economic crisis and shifting attitudes about CSR to incorporate sustainability into the performance of the marketing mix. As a result, "green marketing" has emerged as a distinct school of thought in the field (Gurau & Ranchhod, 2005). Businesses that adopt a green marketing perspective demonstrate to their stakeholders a commitment to environmental responsibility. Considerable demands can be seen coming from both the outside environment (authorities, competitors, customers) and from within (efficiency, competitive superiority). Organizational shifts, including the adoption of green marketing tactics, are being made by hotels in response to internal and external pressures to become more environmentally responsible. However, on a broader level, the adoption of green marketing is not limited to specific activities of a function of the organization; rather, it represents a paradigm shift applied to all employees of the organization, who must come to terms with the interconnectedness of their workplace, the natural world, and the larger community (Rani & Kaur, 2019). As a result, the hotel industry as a whole

Ibrahim Osman, Mohammed Majeed, Esther Asiedu, Jonas Yomboi & Ebenezer Malcalm

must work on embracing green marketing, rather than just the marketing department. The shift in consumer behavior toward making purchasing decisions based on environmental concerns necessitates hotels to adopt green marketing practices (Leonidou *et al.*, 2013). Furthermore, the marketing function serves as the hotel's calling card, as it is the first to reassure guests that the establishment is committed to sustainable practices. In most nations, the hospitality industry is subject to minimal regulatory oversight for environmental concerns (Leonidou *et al.*, 2013). Many hotels, however, are taking proactive measures to improve their environmental performance through the adoption of voluntary programs, practices, ecological initiatives, and green marketing activities (Hussain *et al.*, 2020). Numerous studies have highlighted the importance of adapting marketing strategies to reflect the growing environmental consciousness of consumers. There appears to be a case of marketing myopia at work in the sector of durable goods promotion, with most shifts in approach being more superficial than substantive. This trend suggests that businesses are merely adjusting their marketing communications to create the impression that they are embracing green marketing methods (Thakur & AlSaleh, 2018). In fact, there appears to be widespread ambiguity about what really constitutes "green" in marketing (Mathur *et al.*, 2018). Several critical success elements for implementing green marketing into a company have been identified in the literature. As the topic of environmental sustainability gains prominence, many people are discussing how it affects various aspects of their daily lives, including their consumption habits and the disposal of items they no longer need. Companies are increasingly adopting environmentally friendly advertising and marketing strategies to influence consumer decisions. The primary objective of this chapter is to investigate the elements that influence green marketing, providing vital insights to businesses about the potential effects of these aspects.

This chapter provides researchers and marketing professionals with a thorough examination of the considerations that inform the decision to adopt a green marketing focus. Literature reviews have revealed that both internal and external factors might influence a company's decision to adopt a green marketing strategy. All other aspects are either direct or indirect, and their controllability varies accordingly. Researchers and managers can leverage the chapter's findings by adopting a green marketing approach. This research could inform producers that they must adhere to recently enacted laws mandating the use of ethical production methods while developing environmentally friendly products.

LITERATURE

Green Marketing

To generate and facilitate a form of trade where people's requirements are met with minimal impact on the planet's resources, "green marketing" encompasses a wide range of marketing operations and tactics designed to inspire and maintain environmentally conscious consumers' views and behaviors (Chen & Chang, 2013). These changes represent a widespread effort in today's commercial world, including the hotel industry, to secure long-term growth and consider the interplay between companies, communities, and the natural world. The company must consider natural reasonableness, social ideals, and sustainability in order to maintain the environment. It is also important to draw lines between moral and immoral behavior. As a result, while green marketing may have seemed like a radical concept a few years ago, it is now an absolute necessity if we are to rescue our planet. In addition, Nguyen *et al.*(2019) identified the growing recognition that environmental imbalance poses a significant threat to human survival as a notable shift in consumer behavior. The motivation behind marketing durable goods is being shaped by an increasing understanding of health problems, a desire to give back to nature, a sense of altruism, growing awareness of behavioral and response notions, and an interest in taking actions that benefit the environment. The incorporation of "green marketing practices" into consumer goods is expected to include a protracted process that begins with product certification and extends to modifications to the product's characteristics, logistics, initial material selections, packaging-based inventiveness (Dubihlela & Ngxukumeshe, 2016), and retail-based advertising opportunities (Lingam *et al.*, 2022). Employees can be attracted to and kept by a company that is actively striving toward sustainable development, as noted by Rani and Kaur (2019). People who recycle, go paperless, drive hybrid cars, reduce water usage, and take steps to preserve energy are seen as innovative and knowledgeable.

FACTORS DETERMINING THE ADOPTION OF GREEN MARKETING

In today's market, companies that make an effort to be more environmentally friendly are seen as forward-thinking and innovative (Dangelico & Pontrandolfo, 2010). Market prospects, environmental legislation, competitive constraints, and a sense of social responsibility are all major factors propelling the rise of green marketing (Mishra & Sharma, 2010). New environmental considerations and other elements are included in the conventional marketing mix (4Ps of marketing). The focus is also given to product, pricing, marketing, and distribution of eco-friendly goods. According to AlFuqaha and AlSaifi (2015), these elements include laws aimed at preserving the environment, a scarcity of raw materials, shifts in consumer preferences, and the views of upper management on green advertising. Moreover, the extent to which the food industry has adopted green marketing remains a subject of interest.

Internal Factors

Attitudes of Owners - Managers

Managers' concern for environmental attitudes, such as the physical environment, is worthy of protection, understanding, or enhancement (Laroche *et al.*, 2001). Attitudes toward change and the environment, knowledge of the benefits of green practices, perception and relationship with the external environment, and organizational variables like size, company location, and financial situation all play a role in whether or not firms and managers are concerned about the environment and are willing to take action on this concern (Bohdanowicz, 2005).

Cost

Companies are incorporating green marketing strategies into their cost-cutting strategies. Several potential outcomes may arise: a company may develop expertise in waste reduction, which it can then license to others or apply to its own recycling processes. Significant cost savings can result from reducing hazardous waste. In some cases, businesses form mutually beneficial partnerships in which one company's waste becomes a low-cost resource for another. Fly ash from thermal power plants, for instance, is recycled into bricks that can be utilized in building rather than adding to the enormous amount of solid waste. Although initial investment in green marketing infrastructure is significant due to the development and acceptance of new technologies, these costs will inevitably decline, resulting in increased profitability and long-term viability.

Views of Top-Level Management

Managers are constantly looking for new ways to boost their company's social performance (Dibb *et al.*, 2005) and sustainable performance (Dibb *et al.*, 2005). One of the key pillars for implementing green marketing strategies is senior management's directives towards sustainable development and social responsibility (AlFuqaha & AlSaifi, 2015). Managers need to understand how sustainability performance impacts the company's long-term profitability.

External Factors

Stakeholder Pressure

Stakeholder pressure, as defined by Isabelle *et al.*(2005), refers to the concerns and requests that stakeholders have for organizations to take specific actions. In an effort to advance their own principles and conventions, various stakeholder constituencies are likely to exert pressure on the organization and one another. Those with the most challenging dependencies tend to wield the greatest power within organizations. Even in organizations with strong principles and standards, these factors are sometimes not enough to guarantee environmentally responsible actions. Zhu and Sarkis (2007) argued that organizations conform to normative demands in order to be perceived as more credible. According to the stakeholder theory (Rani & Kaur, 2019), managers should balance the many, and sometimes competing, interests of the organization's constituents. As it provides a framework, *Stakeholder Theory* is well-suited for environmental marketing, as it enables industrial marketers to craft a plan that achieves both the firm's objectives and those of its stakeholders.

Competitive Pressure

Companies' need to stay competitive has also been a driving factor in the development of environmental marketing strategies. Many businesses learn about environmentally conscious practices by observing how their competitors market themselves. Competition has prompted certain industries to modify their practices and reduce their environmental impact.

Consumer Mindset

Customers' purchasing decisions are influenced by several factors, but the nature of the product itself is the most fundamental one (Rani & Kaur, 2019). Other factors, such as a lack of product transparency, high prices, and legal developments, also pose problems. Incidentally, factors, such as security, remuneration, routine concerns, information, age, sexual orientation, attitude, values, brand naming, packaging, and others, all influence consumer concerns and ultimately motivate the purchase of environmentally friendly products. Consumers' attitudes will be treated as knowledge work, meaning they are shaped by how individuals form their beliefs about an organization, which in turn influences their subsequent buying behavior toward green products (a topic that has shown up differently in relation to buyer care in developed nations; Manveer Kaur *et al.*, 2018). Consumers want businesses to act ethically and sustainably, and they will not support brands that harm the environment (Widyastuti & Santoso, 2016). Companies feel significant pressure from this type of legislation, and consumers feel the effects of that legislation when they change their purchasing habits as a result. Setting new goals to improve customer satisfaction requires an emphasis on communicating the social, environmental, and ethical benefits of products to target audiences (Kirgiz, 2016).

Perceived Benefits

There are monetary and non-monetary benefits that businesses can reap by implementing environmental management. Increased revenues, cost savings, and a competitive edge are just a few of the benefits of embracing environmental management (Majeed, 2022). The use of environmental management can also lead to a cleaner and safer workplace, as well as reduced emissions, water usage, and energy costs.

Business Potentials

According to a study by Rani and Kaur (2019), adapting to shifting consumer preferences might provide businesses with an edge over rivals that promote less sustainable products.

Legitimization

The adoption of social and economic (stakeholder) pressure on the corporation through environmentally responsible practices is an example of legitimization. ISO 14001 certification for environmental management helps businesses gain credibility in the eyes of the public and environmentally conscious customers. It is worth noting that, in terms of significance, financial savings are secondary to other environmental goals. Although environmental protection has improved due to regulatory legislation, tensions have arisen between environmental and economic goals. Therefore, there should be a number of criteria applied to the general environmental protection strategies (Carcasov *et al.*, 2017), such as the extent to which they provide positive support in industry; their role in achieving environmental objectives; their effectiveness in terms of social cost; their contribution to providing necessary information to government agencies; and their ease of application and control.

CSR

Companies are increasingly recognizing that they have a responsibility to act in a socially and environmentally responsible manner, as they are part of the larger community. As a result, an increasing number of businesses are adopting the view that they must prioritize both environmental and financial goals. This causes environmental concerns to become an integral part of the company's ethos. Social responsibility is another factor contributing to the adoption of green marketing strategies (Mishra & Sharma, 2010). Babiak and Trendafilova (2011) stated that "the natural environment is increasingly being viewed as a pillar of social responsibility," which lends credence to this argument. Corporate social responsibility (CSR) encompasses ethical purchasing, transparent business procedures, and eco-friendly waste management (Rani & Kaur, 2019). Marketers employ social responsibility not only to boost a company's environmental credibility but also to attract and retain customers (Dhar & Das, 2012). To boost their brand's reputation, several businesses are touting their eco-friendly marketing campaigns (Rani & Kaur, 2019).

Scarcity of Natural Resources

Growing concerns over the impact of current energy production systems, increased energy consumption, and high worldwide demand for limited energy supplies have made energy consumption one of the primary problems of global economic and environmental systems (Caprita, 2015; Kirgiz, 2016). The sales and production of renewable energy are hindered by general factors and government systems. Several factors, including rising prices and taxes on resources, such as gas, electricity, fuel, and timber, have made it more expensive and difficult for businesses to obtain the raw materials they need to carry out their production processes. For this reason, green marketing is being addressed as a pressing issue in today's society (AlFuqaha & AlSaifi, 2015).

Social Media

These days, social networking platforms are indispensable for both personal and professional use. Effective and rapid communication between internet users is made possible by online or electronic media. Organizations can gain insights into their customers' wants and needs through the usage of social media for environmentally friendly projects (Siddique & Hossain, 2018), as well as strengthen their connections with environmentally conscious clientele. According to Siddique and Hossain (2018), social media is a crucial avenue through which consumers can learn about green products and develop environmentally conscious attitudes. Siddique and Hossain (2018) found that the effect of social media on green product awareness is inconclusive. However, prior studies have stated that social media, specifically green blogging, has inspired and impacted people to make environmentally friendly decisions (Biswas, 2016). AlFuqaha and AlSaifi (2015) found that when consumers have easy access to reliable information about a company, they are more likely to purchase environmentally friendly products.

Government

The government typically coerces businesses into adopting consumer-friendly policies. This is achieved through measures, such as reducing the production of harmful items or by-products, adjusting how customers and businesses use and consume hazardous products, and ensuring that consumers of all backgrounds can evaluate products based on their environmental impact (Rani & Kaur, 2019). The government's desire to "protect" consumers and society is a driving force behind many green marketing initiatives. On a broader scale, government restrictions are forcing businesses to implement green marketing strategies (Hale, 2011). Green marketing policies are implemented by governments to protect consumers from exposure to potentially harmful products and to assist consumers in evaluating the environmental impact of green products. While many countries have made significant advances in enacting and enforcing environmental legislation, Dauvergne and Lister (2012) caution that this progress is sometimes hindered by the lack of a global framework for enforcing environmental regulations and standards, with no internationally enforced environmental regulations in place. As most countries worldwide have laws to protect consumers and the environment from hazardous goods or by-products, governmental pressure to become more environmentally responsible is increasing. To encourage corporate social responsibility, the government issues businesses with a variety of environmental permits.

Ecological Concern

Global warming, pollution, and consumer health are just a few of today's social and environmental concerns (Kaur & Bhatia, 2018). Products that are safe for the environment and the planet are more appealing to them (Mobrezi & Khoshtinat, 2016). Consumers' concern for the environment is related to their product knowledge and their interest in purchasing green or eco-friendly products. Consumers who care about the environment are more likely to buy eco-friendly goods (Kianpour, Anvari, Jusoh, & Othman, 2014). However, Siddique and Hossain (2018) found that customers' awareness of green products is not influenced by environmental concern. According to Joshi and Rahman (2015), positive environmental views have not been found to affect the purchasing of green items in the past. Chekima, Wafa, Igau, & Chekima (2015) and Sharma (2017) found that people who care about environmental issues are more likely to make environmentally conscious purchases.

IMPLICATIONS

The chapter has numerous implications. Managers must reduce the production, sale, and use of potentially hazardous products. They ensure that everyone who makes a purchase can assess its impact on the environment. In an effort to reduce waste, many businesses must reassess their manufacturing methods. In such circumstances, they frequently devise more efficient production procedures that reduce waste and eliminate the need for specific raw materials. As a result, they save money on both disposal fees and raw materials. Both producers and marketers will benefit from the findings of this chapter, as they will help them realize that consumers are willing to spend money on environmentally friendly products, provided they are priced affordably. It is essential for manufacturers and retailers of eco-friendly products to remember that customers often prefer stores that are conveniently located near their homes. Moreover, customers are more likely to switch to or remain loyal to a company if it offers a wide selection of products with various advantages.

Interest in environmentalism and efforts to standardize green marketing strategies are expected to remain buoyed by concerns over climate change and global warming. Marketers are investing in long-term green marketing activities to continue supplying cutting-edge green products, anticipating the industry's rapid expansion with an anticipated increase in interest in environmentally friendly goods. However, certain aspects of green marketing are beyond the control of most businesses. Organizational culture, internal processes, and the marketing machinery are all found to be controllable. Additionally, it appears that some other aspects, such as the organization's size, employee pressure, and partners' willingness to engage in green activities, are also within management's control, while others, like the weather, are not. The list of green marketing factors presented in this chapter is not intended to be exhaustive. Other elements may need to be added, or some of the specified ones removed, depending on environmental conditions or different business models. Future studies in this area will likely build on a combination of controllable, semi-controllable, and uncontrollable characteristics attributed to the external and internal environments, as well as to specific stakeholders. Adopting green marketing methods across all consumer-facing businesses will be difficult. Companies are attempting to adopt environmentally friendly advertising strategies, but doing so will be a challenge. The literature findings of this chapter highlight the significance of customers' environmental concerns and environmental literacy in raising their awareness of the negative impacts of using non-green products. Managers will learn that green products are not only beneficial for people's health but also for the environment, and that a healthy, sustainable ecosystem is essential to human life.

CONCLUSION

The findings of this research suggest that the adoption of green practices is positively influenced by owner-manager attitudes, environmental awareness, and the presence of competitors. Compliance with environmental legislation, the goal of achieving sustainable competitive advantage, fulfillment of corporate social responsibility obligations, pressure from environmental activists, and the rise of green consumerism are the primary motivations driving corporations to adopt green marketing strategies. The reviewed literature also emphasizes the importance of viewing environmental responsibility (or 'greening') as just one aspect of the broader marketing function.

REFERENCES

Al Fuqaha, P., Al Saifi, M. (2015). Factors influencing the level of adoption of food industry companies for sustainable marketing in Palestine. *ordan Journal of Business Administration, 11*(2), 381-409.

Biswas, A. (2016). Impact of social media usage factors on green consumption behavior based on technology acceptance model. *Journal of Advanced Management Science, 4*(2), 92-97.
[http://dx.doi.org/10.12720/joams.4.2.92-97]

Caprita, D. (2015). The importance of green marketing for the future businesses *Competitiveness of Agro - Food & Environmental Economy,* 242-254.

Dauvergne, P., Lister, J. (2012). Big brand sustainability: Governance prospects and environmental limits. *Global Environmental Change, 22*(1), 36-45.
[http://dx.doi.org/10.1016/j.gloenvcha.2011.10.007]

Dubihlela, J., Ngxukumeshe, T. (2016). Eco-friendly retail product attributes, customer attributes and the repurchase intentions of South African consumers. *International Business & Economics Research Journal, 15*(4), 163-174. [IBER].
[http://dx.doi.org/10.19030/iber.v15i4.9754]

Kirgiz, A. (2016). *The Marketing Book.*. Basingstoke, United Kingdom: Palgrave Macmillan.

Laroche, M., Bergeron, J., Barbaro-Forleo, G. (2001). Targeting consumers who are willing to pay more for environmentally friendly products. *Journal of Consumer Marketing, 18*(6), 503-520.
[http://dx.doi.org/10.1108/EUM0000000006155]

Lingam, N., Aishwarya, M., Smruti, M.M., Rabi, N.S. (2022). Retail format choice for smartphone purchase: Online *versus* offline. *Horizon Journal of Humanities & Social Sciences Research, 4*(S), 75-88.

Gurău, C., Ranchhod, A. (2005). International green marketing. *International Marketing Review, 22*(5), 547-561.
[http://dx.doi.org/10.1108/02651330510624381]

Hale, T. (2011). A Climate Coalition of the Willing. *Wash. Q., 34*(1), 89-101.
[http://dx.doi.org/10.1080/0163660X.2011.534971]

Mishra, P., Sharma, P. (2010). Green Marketing in India: Opportunities and Challenges. *Journal of Engineering Science & Management Education, 3*(1), 9-14.

Mathur, S., Valecha, R.R., Khanna, V. (2018). A Study on the Impact of Green Marketing on Consumer Buying Behavior in Automobile Industry. *International Journal for Advance Research and Development, 3*(1), 286-290.

Nguyen, H.V., Nguyen, N., Nguyen, B.K., Lobo, A., Vu, P.A. (2019). Organic food purchases in an emerging market: The influence of consumers' personal factors and green marketing practices of food stores. *International journal of Environmental Research and Public Health, 16*(6), 1037.
[http://dx.doi.org/10.3390/ijerph16061037] [PMID: 30909390]

Rani, A., Kaur, P. (2019). Factors Affecting the Adoption of Green Lifestyle in Indian Environment. *Journal of Emerging Technologies and Innovative Research , 6*(6), 762-769.

Thakur, R., AlSaleh, D. (2018). A comparative study of corporate user-generated media behavior: Cross-cultural B2B context. *Industrial Marketing Management, 73*, 125-136. [http://dx.doi.org/10.1016/j.indmarman.2018.02.004]

Widyastuti, S., Santoso, B. (2016). Green marketing. *ASEAN Marketing Journal, 8*(8), 104-115.

CHAPTER 6

Green Packaging

Abstract: Sustainable packaging is on the rise as businesses become increasingly aware of the need to minimize their negative impact on the environment. Sustainable packaging refers to the practice of creating packages that are environmentally friendly without compromising functionality. Sustainable packaging can reduce the environmental impact of manufacturing by minimizing waste and pollution, while also lowering operational costs. This chapter examines three key areas: types of green packaging, the benefits of green packaging, and the challenges of green packaging.

Keywords: Environment, Green, Marketing, Packaging, Sustainable.

INTRODUCTION

Sustainable packaging, also known as "green packaging," is gaining attention from academics and industry professionals worldwide. Companies are developing novel lines of products for sustainable, reusable packaging, which necessitates either the installation of new filling lines to accommodate the new packaging types or the formation of a partnership with packaging suppliers (Wandosell *et al.,* 2021). The use of sustainable packaging solutions has moved beyond the voluntary stage. Sustainable packaging techniques are increasingly being required of enterprises by government requirements, consumer preferences, and corporate standards. These concerns about the environment are driving the adoption of greener packaging options, which could ultimately result in cost savings for businesses in the long run (Shah, 2022). It appears that businesses are cognizant of the need for sustainable packaging; nevertheless, internal and external constraints may prevent them from fully embracing these practices (de Koeijer *et al.*, 2017). Environmental and cost-based regulations on packaging procedures provide challenges that have been studied in the past (Afif *et al.*, 2022). Adoption barriers to green packaging, such as the packaging used by stores, have also been studied in research. This chapter examines three key areas: types of green packaging, the benefits of green packaging, and the challenges of green packaging.

Ibrahim Osman, Mohammed Majeed, Esther Asiedu, Jonas Yomboi & Ebenezer Malcalm

LITERATURE

Theoretical Framework: Guiding Perspectives on Sustainable Packaging

This chapter draws on two foundational theories—Stakeholder Theory and the Triple Bottom Line Framework—to critically examine the strategic role of sustainable packaging in contemporary business environments. These theoretical lenses provide the conceptual grounding necessary for understanding how green packaging aligns with both corporate objectives and societal expectations.

Stakeholder Theory (Freeman, 1984)

Stakeholder Theory posits that the success of a business depends on its ability to manage relationships with a wide array of stakeholders, including consumers, employees, regulators, investors, and advocacy groups. Unlike the traditional shareholder-centric view, this theory emphasizes broader accountability. Sustainable packaging is a strategic response to the rising expectations of these diverse stakeholders. For example, environmentally conscious consumers demand reduced plastic use, while regulators impose stricter waste management policies. Investors are increasingly considering ESG (Environmental, Social, and Governance) performance in their investment decisions, and NGOs are exerting pressure through campaigns and audits. By adopting green packaging solutions, firms demonstrate responsiveness to these stakeholders, thereby enhancing legitimacy, brand reputation, and long-term viability.

Triple Bottom Line (Elkington, 1997)

The Triple Bottom Line framework expands the definition of corporate success beyond financial profitability to include social equity and environmental stewardship. This "people, planet, profit" approach advocates for a holistic performance metric. Sustainable packaging directly contributes to this model by reducing environmental harm (*e.g.*, through the use of biodegradable materials), improving social outcomes (*e.g.*, through fair trade and ethical sourcing practices), and maintaining economic efficiency (*e.g.*, through cost savings resulting from material reduction). Organizations that integrate sustainable packaging into their operations signal their commitment to responsible business practices across all three dimensions, thereby reinforcing their sustainability credentials and future-proofing their brand. Together, these theories establish a solid analytical foundation for assessing how sustainable packaging is not merely a technical or operational decision but a strategic imperative shaped by complex external pressures and internal value commitments.

GREEN PACKAGING

In order to ensure that products are both efficient and secure for people and for the environment, "green packaging," also known as "eco-green packaging," "eco-friendly packaging," "sustainable packaging," or "recyclable packaging," employs environmentally friendly materials for packaging purposes. Green packaging refers to packagings that have a minimal impact on the natural world. This is accomplished through the utilization of renewable energy sources and the use of environmentally friendly resources (such as recyclable or biodegradable containers and packaging features) (Owens, 2019). In a nutshell, environmentally conscious packaging means being conscientious of the company's impact on the environment.

TYPES OF GREEN PACKAGING

Packaging Made from Mushrooms

Mycelium, the root-like structure of mushrooms, is used to bind together agricultural waste in mushroom-based packaging. Though it may sound like an experimental wrap from a vegan restaurant, mushroom packaging has proven effective in commercial applications. Mycelium-based materials are formed by growing the fungus around agricultural waste, creating a strong, biodegradable packaging solution that is environmentally friendly and breaks down quickly.

Biodegradable Packaging / Compostable Containers

The materials used in this package are biodegradable. This packaging does not need to decompose within a certain amount of time in order to be considered biodegradable. Biodegradable packaging has the advantage of being completely non-polluting after it has decomposed. Biodegradable packaging refers to any type of packaging that can be decomposed into harmless or useful substances, such as water, carbon dioxide, or compost, by the action of microorganisms, fungi, or enzymes from the environment. Paper, cardboard, starch, cellulose, and biopolymers are just a few of the elements that can be used to create biodegradable packaging. The use of biodegradable packaging is beneficial to the circular economy, as it helps reduce the amount of plastic waste that ends up in landfills, oceans, and incinerators. There are several ways in which biodegradable packaging can help businesses, consumers, and the planet. Biodegradable packaging offers numerous environmental benefits, including reduced greenhouse gas emissions, conservation of energy and resources, and the avoidance of pollution and biodiversity loss. It also provides social advantages, such as improved public health, increased green job opportunities, and greater awareness of waste reduction and recycling. For businesses, biodegradable packaging can lower environmental impact, reduce disposal costs, and minimize regulatory risks.

Starch-Based Biomaterial

In particular, packaging made from cornstarch has experienced a meteoric rise in popularity during the past decade. Cornstarch-based packaging is substantially more sustainable than plastic packaging despite sharing many of plastic's features. Soda bottling technology and loose-fill packaging are just two examples of how manufacturers can apply starch-based biomaterials.

Recyclable or Environmentally Friendly Packaging

Cardboard, glass, and paper are the first materials that come to mind when considering recyclable packaging. There is no doubt that these materials are recyclable. However, these days, recycling is not limited to simply cardboard, paper, and glass; many more materials can also be recycled. Materials that can be recycled are counted among those that can be used again. The term "recycling" refers to the process of converting waste materials into new materials and products. To be recognized as environmentally friendly, a package must meet the following four criteria: materials are sourced, transported, and produced using renewable energy; the materials themselves are recyclable; the package contains no harmful contaminants or chemicals; and the product is recyclable.

Reusable Packaging

After its initial use, this type of container can be reused for other purposes. For example, cardboard boxes can serve both as delivery containers and later for storing items after an online purchase. Glass jars are another common form of reusable packaging.

Sustainable Packaging

Eco-friendly packaging refers to packaging that is environmentally friendly. This pertains not just to the packaging itself, but also to the method used to design such packaging and the materials employed in its construction.

Compostable

As it decomposes without leaving behind any toxic chemicals, compostable packaging has gained popularity. Compostable packaging is typically crafted from corn, sugar cane, carrots, and beets.

Reduced Packaging

Reduced packaging refers to the practice of minimizing the amount of packaging used for a product. Die-cut cardboard boxes offer a practical alternative to bulky boxes filled with packing peanuts. Made from corrugated cardboard, these boxes provide cushioning during transit while using less material.

BENEFITS OF GREEN PACKAGING

Biodegradable

If packaging is made from organic materials, it can naturally break down in the environment. Plastic is not readily biodegradable and can take hundreds to thousands of years to decompose, releasing toxic compounds in the process. Composting will be an option for some environmentally friendly packaging, such as sustainable paper products.

Reduces Carbon Imprint

The most obvious advantage of eco-friendly packaging pertains to environmental safety. To lessen its impact on the environment, eco-friendly packaging typically employs biodegradable or recycled materials. The process of production is also typically improved, saving valuable resources and lowering the adverse effects that companies have on their surroundings. Environmental consciousness is becoming increasingly important to consumers, which has a direct impact on the products and companies they choose to support. Companies can demonstrate their commitment to social responsibility and send a message to their target market by switching to environmentally friendly packaging for their products and lessening the use of nonrenewable energy sources. To minimize its environmental impact, "green" packaging generates as little waste as possible during production (Bulk Bag Reclamation, 2019).

Raise Revenues

Consumers are increasingly drawn to products that help them reduce their environmental impact. Today's merchants face growing pressure to minimize their ecological footprint, making sustainable packaging a priority. Customers who recognize that the packaging they choose lowers their carbon footprint are not only more likely to buy those products but also to recommend them to their environmentally conscious friends (Paramount Packaging, 2021).

Decrease in the Use of Renewable Resources

Manufacturers of "green" packaging contribute to a more sustainable world by producing products with a low environmental impact. This reduction is important because it helps ensure that Earth's resources remain available for future generations (Bulk Bag Reclamation, 2019). The use of green packaging can also reduce the energy required to produce and package products. By switching to biodegradable packaging, companies can decrease waste, water use, energy consumption, and pollution. This not only benefits the environment but also lowers costs by reducing the amount of packaging needed. Over time, these savings can make the transition to sustainable packaging financially worthwhile for businesses.

Advantages for the Environment

Sustainable packaging typically employs the use of recycled materials, which reduces manufacturing waste. The company using sustainable packaging will have fewer adverse effects on the environment due to its more efficient production method.

Increasing Reliance on Recyclable Materials

Creating new packaging requires a significant amount of energy and resources, so recycling as much as possible helps conserve both. Products made from recycled materials consume less energy and water than their brand-new counterparts. The use of 100% post-consumer recycled paper products and recycled plastics are examples of goals that green packaging aims to achieve (Bulk Bag Reclamation, 2019).

Enhances Company Reputation

The more environmentally conscious a business appears, the more loyal its customers tend to be. Companies that offer adaptable, eco-friendly packaging can build credibility as ethical merchants. Paramount Packaging's Green line of products provides an excellent way for businesses to demonstrate their commitment to ethical, environmental, and social responsibility (Paramount Packaging, 2021).

Creates a Bigger Market

Customers who value eco-friendly policies are more likely to become repeat buyers. As the movement toward sustainability gains momentum, consumers increasingly prefer to do business with companies committed to sustainable practices and goals (Shah, 2022).

Improved Production Techniques

Green packaging aims to employ renewable energy sources like wind and solar instead of fossil fuels (Bulk Bag Reclamation, 2019). The use of renewable resources has increased; for example, many eco-friendly packagers have switched from using paper made from trees to utilizing paper made from agricultural fibers.

Simple Disposal

The packaging selected can be of any type, but it must be recyclable or biodegradable. Waste packaging can be converted into compost if clients or colleagues have access to composting facilities. Recyclable packaging, as indicated by the recycling symbol, can be discarded in the recycling bin. Consumers can more easily dispose of items packaged in recyclable, compostable, or biodegradable materials. It gives them greater flexibility in terms of where and how to dispose of these items, and businesses should continually strive to make their products easy to use. This philosophy is exemplified through biodegradable materials. Composting-friendly consumers, for instance, will not have to alter their trash disposal habits. Like any other compost-friendly material, they can incorporate biodegradable packaging into their compost to increase the product's overall value.

Conserves Resources

Much of the trash that pollutes our ecosystems comes from packages. Choosing a sustainable alternative will reduce the amount of waste dumped into waterways, forests, and oceans. Sustainable packaging items are not only created from lightweight, nearly 100% recyclable materials, but are also designed to enhance food safety, increase shelf life, and reduce food waste. The employment of technology that maintains food's freshness for longer is made possible by biomaterials. The longer shelf life is intended to reduce food waste in the food service industry as a whole. The film's ability to lock in food's freshness and prevent spoilage is just one of the ways bio-materials benefit the business (Paramount Packaging, 2021).

Eco-Friendly Packaging

Eco-friendly containers are adaptable and can be utilized in any sector where conventional packaging is prevalent. The versatility of these materials makes them a great alternative to more conventional forms of packaging. Not only does conventional packaging harm the environment, but it also stifles innovation in the packaging industry. When it comes to environmentally responsible packaging, businesses will have more freedom to experiment with novel shapes and designs.

Additionally, most food items can be packaged in environmentally friendly materials without risk to the consumer's health.

Saving Money on Shipping

If firms can reduce transportation costs, time and money can be saved by using fewer raw materials for product packaging. Investing in a paper shredder is a smart choice for disposing of used packaging in an eco-friendly way. Regardless of how well a package is designed, how easily it can be recycled or composted, or how responsibly its materials are sourced, it will not be a sustainable long-term solution if its production costs are too high. Cost is often overlooked during the packaging design process, despite playing a critical role in determining whether a new packaging concept is commercially viable.

Brand Image Enhancement

Eco-friendly packaging enhances a company's reputation. Customers who recognize a business's commitment to environmental preservation tend to have a more favorable impression of the company overall. This strengthened brand recognition can positively impact both the company's bottom line and return on investment.

CHALLENGES OF GREEN PACKAGING

Communication Restrictions

Limitations on communication include being unable to connect with suppliers or assess how well employees are performing their jobs. Insufficient or nonexistent communication across departments is a common barrier to implementing sustainable procurement strategies (Koberg & Longoni, 2019; Majumdar & Sinha, 2019). The sustainable development department's ideals and the supply chain's implementation of those ideas may not always align (Boks, 2006). For instance, the sustainability team may not collaborate with the marketing and sales teams on the creation of promotional and environmentally friendly initiatives.

Problems with Costs

Creating environmentally friendly packaging can be time-consuming and expensive. Sustainable packaging is now more expensive than traditional packaging, as it should be. This is due to the use of virgin and recycled materials, as well as the lack of a well-established supply chain, less efficient manufacturing techniques, and smaller economies of scale. Companies often lack the necessary funds to invest in research and development for improved packaging, according to

Afif *et al.*(2022). Many companies, especially those on a smaller scale, find it prohibitively expensive to move to environmentally friendly packaging. The change in packaging may increase the cost of production as well as the cost of any internal packaging procedures that are affected. It may be challenging to predict exactly when eco-friendly packaging options will become cost-effective.

Contamination

Eco-friendly packaging utilizes materials that decompose quickly, provided they are disposed of properly. Cross-contamination is a significant issue with packaging at both the consumer and recycling levels. Eco-friendly packaging that has been contaminated by other materials may be rejected by recycling centers, leading to increased trash and a larger carbon footprint for businesses.

Improving the Durability of Materials to Preserve Contents

Packaging made from sustainable materials must be as effective as packaging made from non-sustainable materials. Food waste and/or product damage are additional concerns beyond simply satisfying customers' expectations. Packaging's primary purpose is to safeguard the contents, hence any skimping on security is unacceptable.

Time-Consuming

Some seasonal agricultural crops are needed to produce sustainable packaging materials. Corn, as an example, is both an expensive and renewable crop. Corn is used not just for food but also for compostable packaging. Some have proposed using it as a food substitute instead of packaging, which would benefit the world's poorest populations.

Some Packaging Materials Could Be Dangerous

Sustainable packaging may not be foolproof against cross-contamination in grocery stores and markets. They are missing crucial qualities for maintaining the product's security. Nothing is more valuable than a human life, so we must never put it at risk by ignoring this consideration.

Constraints on Resources

Both money and time are limited due to the budget constraints. There are many facets to costs that can act as a barrier. The initial prices of sustainable packaging can be prohibitive, preventing its widespread use (Wang *et al.*, 2016). This is consistent with the broader widespread perception that businesses lack the resources to invest in sustainability (Wang *et al.*, 2016) and the fact that they believe sustainability adoption to be too expensive (Silvestre *et al.*, 2018). Additionally, businesses may find that the adoption of sustainable practices falls short of their expectations for financial returns on investment (Irani *et al.*, 2017; Silvestre *et al.*, 2018). At the very least, dating back a few years, this has been considered a commercial drawback.

SOLUTIONS TO CHALLENGES OF GREEN PACKAGING

Reduce

Thinner and stronger materials can do the same task with less bulk (Lawson, 2017). Businesses can reduce the amount of raw materials used in production, as well as the amount of energy used in processing and storing finished goods.

Reuse

An increasing number of items, such as boxes with specialized coatings to enhance durability, are available to facilitate reuse. Taking advantage of reuse capabilities can save money in the long run (Lawson, 2017). Packaging for auto parts is one example of a reusable product that businesses may design. Making the most of a product's lifespan is just as important as reducing its packaging footprint. Reusable packaging is exactly what it sounds like: packaging designed to be used multiple times. This includes bulk and handheld containers made from durable materials, as well as pallets and shipping racks. Reusable containers can be made from a wide range of long-lasting materials, including wood, metals, and plastics.

Renew

Several criteria must be met before packaging can be considered "renewable." All of the energy used in its production, transportation, and storage must come from renewable sources. Biodegradable packaging that can also be composted or used to produce renewable energy is ideal. Moreover, if it is well-manufactured, it can also be repurposed for other types of packaging.

Repurpose

If certain products or materials within a company can be refused, reduced, or reused, taking those steps is essential. At the core of "repurposing" is the practice of reusing materials originally intended for a different purpose. Among environmentally conscious individuals, this is often referred to as "upcycling," which typically requires creative problem-solving. For example, cardboard boxes or other packaging materials from a job site can be saved and reused for storage.

Repurposing as much material as possible contributes to more effective waste management.

Recycle

It is becoming increasingly common for manufacturers to label their products as containing recycled content. This practice not only appeals to environmentally conscious consumers but also helps manufacturers manage rising raw material costs. By reusing scraps of paper, metal, or other materials from previous production runs, companies can reduce waste and production expenses. Additionally, designing products that can be easily disassembled into reusable components further supports sustainable manufacturing practices.

Refuse

Avoid buying food that has traveled a long distance or originated from another country. Avoid taking the easy way out, such as frequenting chain supermarkets. Avoid buying fruits and vegetables that come in excessive or disposable packaging.

CASE STUDIES: SUCCESSES AND FAILURES IN SUSTAINABLE PACKAGING

Sustainable packaging initiatives have seen varying degrees of success across leading global corporations. These case studies of Unilever, Nestlé, and Coca-Cola highlight the complexities and contradictions often involved in aligning environmental goals with operational realities.

Unilever – A Refill Revolution

Unilever's partnership with TerraCycle's Loop program exemplifies an innovative and scalable approach to sustainable packaging. Through the "Refill Revolution," Unilever introduced reusable containers for everyday products like shampoo and detergent. These were made available at branded refill stations in UK supermarkets, allowing customers to return and refill rather than dispose of packaging. This closed-loop system not only reduced plastic waste but also enhanced consumer engagement and loyalty. Unilever's success underscores how infrastructure and consumer convenience can work hand-in-hand to drive sustainable behaviour.

Nestlé – Innovation Without Infrastructure

Nestlé made headlines by introducing recyclable paper-based packaging for its YES! snack bars—an industry first. The move demonstrated bold innovation and garnered positive attention from sustainability advocates. However, criticism soon followed as the packaging's recyclability depended heavily on the availability of proper waste management infrastructure, which is lacking in many regions. This case highlights a common pitfall in sustainable packaging: innovation must be complemented by systemic support, including public infrastructure and consumer education, to fully realize its environmental benefits.

Coca-Cola – Performance *Versus* Pledges

Coca-Cola's pledge to use 50% recycled materials in its packaging by 2030 signals strong long-term sustainability ambitions. However, the company was named the world's top plastic polluter in the 2022 Break Free from Plastic audit—an embarrassing contradiction between aspiration and current practice. While Coca-Cola continues to experiment with plant-based and recyclable bottle prototypes, its high production volumes and reliance on single-use plastics dilute the impact of such innovations. This case reflects the challenge of scale in sustainability; even with strong commitments, real-world results can fall short if production practices do not evolve in tandem.

These cases collectively demonstrate that while sustainable packaging offers a pathway to environmental and reputational benefits, success depends on strategic alignment, supporting systems, and the ability to translate ambition into measurable action.

IMPLICATIONS

Organizations in the production sector might distinguish themselves by portraying themselves as environmentally conscious. Customers are more likely to do business with firms that have a good reputation for protecting the environment. Manufacturers are now under additional pressure to disclose information about the full lifecycle of their products and use environmentally friendly resources in their packaging. Companies that prioritize their bottom line will recognize that environmentally friendly packaging is essential. Sustainable packaging offers numerous advantages for businesses, including lower production costs, smaller carbon footprints, and a more positive public perception of the company's brand (Katun, 2010). At one time, concerns about global warming and biodiversity were limited to a select few. However, worsening environmental conditions, combined with increased awareness driven by advances in communication and technology, have brought these issues to the forefront of public attention in recent years. Customers' perceptions of the businesses they support are shifting as a result of the growing environmental consciousness among the general public. To stay competitive and contribute to environmental preservation, businesses must adapt to meet the evolving needs of their customers, which now include a growing demand for environmentally friendly products. Further study is needed to find solutions that enable more sustainable products, and this may be achieved by identifying the key hurdles that impede firms from utilizing environmentally conscious packaging.

CONCLUSION

This chapter focuses on three crucial aspects of green packaging: the various types of green packaging, the advantages of green packaging, and the difficulties associated with green packaging. Negative repercussions on people and society as a whole have resulted from a lack of environmental consciousness. One way to make the world a better place to live is to shift toward using environmentally friendly packaging. There has been progress in using more environmentally friendly materials for packaging in recent years. Whether the motivation is financial or environmental, switching to eco-friendly packaging offers significant advantages. The benefits of using biodegradable packaging should encourage business owners to adopt more sustainable practices. Beyond surface-level gains, such as reduced costs and lower carbon emissions, companies can also improve consumer convenience and contribute to the reduction of plastic waste. Sustainable packaging can aid in waste minimization and pollution prevention by being designed for reuse or recycling. This has the dual benefit of reducing the quantity of hazardous chemicals and pollutants discharged into the environment, as well as the amount of plastic, paper, and other materials that end up in landfills. Businesses can reduce the time it takes for packaging to disintegrate by switching to biodegradable materials. Looking ahead, it is reasonable to assume that more businesses will adopt environmentally sound procedures once they experience the benefits. With this in mind, the best course of action is to take immediate action; biodegradable packaging is a small but significant step in the right direction. Despite its advantages, biodegradable packaging faces several obstacles that could hinder its widespread adoption. The primary issues are the high cost and limited availability of biodegradable packaging compared to traditional plastic. The performance and quality of biodegradable packaging may also be inferior to those of traditional plastic packaging. Furthermore, there is a lack of uniform standards and certification schemes that can validate and relay the environmental benefits and claims made for biodegradable packaging. As a result of these issues, both consumers and businesses may be deterred from using biodegradable packaging.

REFERENCES

Bulk Bag Reclamation. (2019). What Is Green Packaging? https://bulkbagreclamation.com/what-is-gre-n-packaging/

Afif, K., Rebolledo, C., Roy, J. (2022). Drivers, barriers and performance outcomes of sustainable packaging: a systematic literature review. *British Food Journal.*, *124*(3), 915-935.

[http://dx.doi.org/10.1108/BFJ-02-2021-0150]

Boks, C. (2006). The soft side of ecodesign. *Journal of Cleaner Production., 14*(15-16), 1346-1356.
[http://dx.doi.org/10.1016/j.jclepro.2005.11.015]

Koberg, E., Longoni, A. (2019). A systematic review of sustainable supply chain management in global supply chains. *Journal of Cleaner Production., 207*, 1084-1098.
[http://dx.doi.org/10.1016/j.jclepro.2018.10.033]

Irani, Z., Kamal, M.M., Sharif, A., Love, P.E.D., Irani, Z., Kamal, M.M., Sharif, A., Love, P.E.D. (2017). Enabling sustainable energy futures: factors influencing green supply chain collaboration. *Production Planning & Control., 28*(6-8), 684-705.
[http://dx.doi.org/10.1080/09537287.2017.1309710]

Majumdar, A., Sinha, S.K. (2019). Analyzing the barriers of green textile supply chain management in Southeast Asia using interpretive structural modeling. *Sustainable Production and Consumption, 17*, 176-187.
[http://dx.doi.org/10.1016/j.spc.2018.10.005]

Silvestre, B.S., Monteiro, M.S., Luiz, F., Viana, E. (2018). Challenges for sustainable supply chain management: when stakeholder collaboration becomes conducive to corruption *Journal of Cleaner Production., 194*, 766-776.
[http://dx.doi.org/10.1016/j.jclepro.2018.05.127]

Wang, Z., Mathiyazhagan, K., Xu, L., Diabat, A. (2016). A decision making trial and evaluation laboratory approach to analyze the barriers to Green Supply Chain Management adoption in a food packaging company. *Journal of Cleaner Production., 117*, 19-28.
[http://dx.doi.org/10.1016/j.jclepro.2015.09.142]

Lawson, E. (2017). Advantages of Green Packaging to the Environment. https://greenbusinessbureau.com/blog/10-advantages-of-green-packaging-to-the-environment/

Paramount Packaging. (2021). https://www.paramount.ie/2021/07/5-benefits-of-eco-friendly-packaging/

Pauer, E., Wohner, B., Heinrich, V., Tacker, M. (2019). Assessing the environmental sustainability of food packaging: An extended life cycle assessment including packaging-related food losses and waste and circularity assessment. *Sustainability (Basel), 11*(3), 925.
[http://dx.doi.org/10.3390/su11030925]

Owens, B. (2019). *What is Green Packaging?*.https://noissue.co/blog/blog-what-is-green-packaging/

Shah, K. (2022). Why Switch to Sustainable packaging is crucial for business growth? https://www.linkedin.com/pulse/why-switch-sustainable-packaging-crucial-business-growth-kushal-shah

Wandosell, G., Parra-Meroño, M.C., Alcayde, A., Baños, R. (2021). Green Packaging from Consumer and Business Perspectives. *Sustainability (Basel), 13*(3), 1356.
[http://dx.doi.org/10.3390/su13031356]

CHAPTER 7

Green Marketing Communication

Abstract: Rapid growth in environmental concerns has compelled corporations to implement environmental safeguards. Green communication is a method of spreading awareness about environmental consciousness that helps both businesses and the world around them. Corporate communications, product display and presentation, eco-labeling, and packaging are some of the effective methods of green marketing communication described in the literature. Green communication, when grounded in best practices, can serve as a vital part of eco-conscious businesses.

Keywords: Companies, Communication, Eco, Environment, Green, Marketing.

INTRODUCTION

Green marketing communication comes under the concept of green marketing (GM). Green marketing is defined by Cheema and Shankar (2011) as an all-encompassing approach to advertising that aims to reduce environmental impact throughout the product life cycle. The growing public and corporate awareness of environmental constraints, such as climate change, non-biodegradable solid waste, and pollution, has further fueled this green marketing trend. Although adopting a green marketing approach may seem costly initially, it will ultimately pay off. According to Kusuma *et al.*(2017), "green marketing" can also be understood as a business strategy for achieving organizational objectives by using marketing mix components that prioritize environmental safety. The goal of green marketing is to attract new customers and retain existing ones who value environmental sustainability. Organizations need to focus their efforts on creating green products that meet the demands of the local market, as customer demand for environmentally friendly goods increases (Mogaji *et al.*, 2022). In the context of sustainability, communication is the most potent force for promoting any concept, product, or service. To sensitize and influence consumption patterns in favor of protecting the world, information must be informative, believable, and convincing. Marketers are increasingly aware of the necessity to implement an effective communication strategy in light of the growing importance of customers in terms of responsible or sustainable consumption for sustainable development. According to Trivedi, Trivedi, and Goswami (2018), firms can maintain their customers' interest and involvement by maintaining open lines of communication

Ibrahim Osman, Mohammed Majeed, Esther Asiedu, Jonas Yomboi & Ebenezer Malcalm

with them. Green marketing communication refers to the dissemination of information about a company's efforts to promote environmental sustainability through its marketing activities. Companies that have engaged in "green" activities, as defined by Goel and Sharma (2017), should create green marketing communications that can be exploited as a competitive advantage. According to Puspitasari *et al.*(2021), green marketing has a notable impact and a beneficial influence on consumer perceptions. If more effort is put into green marketing, consumers' opinions of organic foods are likely to improve.

It is well accepted that green marketing communication can affect both consumer behavior and the public's perception of a company. All business communication continues to be scrutinized by a public that is becoming more aware of sustainability. Long-term solutions to this problem may include green communication. Ecological advertising has two primary goals: (1) to introduce customers to the company and the product, so that they become familiar with the merits of utilizing the company's products and the benefits of the firm's environmentally friendly operations, and (2) To persuade customers to go with the product that will not hurt the environment, to alter their impression of it, and to pique their interest in it. Additionally, it informs and directs consumers toward sources of eco-friendly goods and services. However, firms in emerging economies have struggled to fully integrate their marketing communications with a green orientation, so green marketing communication has been underutilized. To promote the use of efficient green integrated marketing communication, this chapter employed a literature review strategy to create a comprehensive framework for green integrated marketing communications.

The Chapter's Contributions

The state of the global socio-ecological system is widely recognized as having a direct impact on the global economy. This chapter provides an in-depth review of the current literature on green marketing communication. This is the first and only comprehensive evaluation of green marketing communication, making it an invaluable resource for researchers and practitioners alike. Green living is on the rise, and this research makes significant contributions to the study of green marketing communication. It adds to the literature by establishing a link between green marketing communication and consumer understanding. Companies are under increasing pressure to adjust their management practices to account for externalities due to a shifting business climate. In order to keep up with the rapid pace of change, businesses and communities must develop novel approaches to problem-solving and organizational structures. It has been argued that to achieve maximum value, businesses must consider not only financial but also ethical and social capital. Aligned with this perspective, there are strong theoretical grounds for believing that ethical employee behavior contributes positively to business success.

LITERATURE

Theoretical Foundations of Green Marketing

Green marketing, which refers to the promotion of environmentally friendly products and practices, is grounded in several theoretical frameworks that help explain consumer behavior and guide organizational strategies toward sustainability. Among the most influential theories underpinning green marketing are the Theory of Planned Behavior (TPB), Stakeholder Theory, and the Resource-Based View (RBV).

The **Theory of Planned Behavior (TPB)**, developed by Ajzen, posits that human behavior is driven by behavioral intentions, which are in turn shaped by attitudes toward the behavior, subjective norms, and perceived behavioral control. Within green marketing, TPB provides a lens to understand how consumers' attitudes toward the environment, the influence of societal norms (such as peer and media pressures), and their perceived ability to make eco-friendly choices impact their purchasing decisions. For instance, a consumer may intend to buy a sustainable product if they believe it benefits the environment (attitude), if their peers support green practices (subjective norms), and if they feel empowered to make such purchases (perceived control).

Stakeholder Theory extends the focus of business decisions beyond shareholders to include all relevant stakeholders, including customers, employees, communities, suppliers, and regulators. In the context of green marketing, this theory underscores the need for businesses to address the environmental concerns of various stakeholder groups. For example, a company that communicates its sustainability efforts transparently and engages its stakeholders in environmental initiatives can build trust, loyalty, and a positive brand image. Effective green marketing thus requires an inclusive strategy that acknowledges and responds to the expectations of all interested parties.

Ultimately, the **Resource-Based View (RBV)** of the firm emphasizes that a sustainable competitive advantage originates from the firm's unique internal resources and capabilities. When applied to green marketing, RBV suggests that an organization's commitment to sustainability—manifested in green technologies, sustainable supply chains, and eco-innovation—can serve as a distinctive competency. Such green initiatives not only enhance environmental performance but also offer a marketing edge by differentiating the company in a competitive market. Together, these theories offer a robust foundation for understanding and implementing green marketing strategies. They illustrate that successful green marketing is not merely about product promotion but involves aligning organizational values, stakeholder interests, and consumer behavior toward the broader goal of environmental sustainability.

GREEN MARKETING COMMUNICATION (GMC)

As part of the marketing mix, "promotion" refers to the interactions between the business and its consumers. Marketing communications encompass both official company statements and customer-generated content. According to Genc (2017), effective communication is crucial for including various internal and external stakeholders in sustainable development initiatives. The most powerful means of influencing and altering consumers' thoughts, choices, and behaviors are the marketing communications instruments at a marketer's disposal. Awareness, education, knowledge, perception, attitude, interest, engagement, preference building, and motivation to purchase are all goals of advertising (Bagdare, 2018). Collaboration information about ecological pledges and efforts made by enterprises to users is an integral part of green promotion. Advertising, direct marketing, public relations, sales promotions, and in-store events are all examples of promotional activities that fall under this category (Fan & Zeng, 2011). When a company engages in "green promotion," it educates its customers about environmental issues in a genuine and authentic manner. When done effectively, green promotion can help spread the word about an organization's commitment to environmental sustainability and its successes to a wide audience (Majeed, 2022). Advertising, corporate public relations, and visual identification are the most common channels for green marketing communication (Ganganaboina & Riaz, 2017). In addition, a company can implement its green marketing strategy through green marketing communication, which involves disseminating information in various formats about the company's environmental activities and the message it wants to convey to consumers. According to Stoica (2021), green marketing communication prioritizes two-way communication with all relevant parties, with the primary goal of informing and educating customers about the social and environmental benefits of the firm and its offerings. Building brand awareness and positioning, releasing new products, boosting revenue, and keeping existing customers satisfied are just a few of the many company objectives that can be advanced through strategic marketing communication (Bagdare, 2018). Sustainability marketing communication can make use of the same elements of the integrated marketing communication mix used in the marketing of consumer goods and services, such as advertising, sales promotion, public relations, personal selling, event marketing, digital marketing, direct marketing, customer relationship management, and so on (Majeed, 2022).

ELEMENTS OF GREEN MARKETING COMMUNICATION

Majeed (2022) identified green marketing communication (GMC) as consisting of green websites, green advertising, green packaging, and green events. Advertising, corporate public relations, visual identification, green labeling and packaging, and environmentally friendly reports are just some of the channels through which businesses can disseminate their green marketing messages (Tan *et al.*, 2022). Additionally, it can be implemented across various platforms, including online communities, websites, print publications, TV and radio advertisements, and print magazines (Ganganaboina & Sana, 2017). All of these outlets spread the word about the environmental and health benefits of being green, hoping to sway consumers to make more eco-friendly choices. Corporate communication, corporate sustainability disclosure, public relations, corporate social responsibility, product advertising, product display and presentation, eco-labeling, and packaging are all successful marketing communication techniques, as stated by Bagdare (2018).

Eco-Friendly Advertising

As a form of marketing communication, green advertising has the potential to meet the needs of ecologically conscious consumers (Ankit & Mayur, 2013). "Promotional messages that can address the needs and desires of consumers interested in the environment" are included in green advertising. Marketing green products emphasizes their positive attributes, such as their low environmental and social impact, long product life, and reduced dependence on finite resources. These messages have an impact on consumers, encouraging them to purchase environmentally friendly products (Chang, 2011). According to the study by Siddique & Hossain (2018), consumers' purchasing decisions are significantly influenced by promotional activities on environmentally friendly items and reference groups. This practice involves addressing the concerns of ecologically aware consumers by incorporating messages that are in harmony with nature (Kumar & Kumar, 2017). Advertisers utilize "green" messaging to frame their goods as environmentally friendly options (Majeed, 2022). Individuals' perceptions of advertising and their propensity to act sustainably are influenced by green marketing campaigns (Kim *et al.*, 2019). Researchers have found that green advertising does have an impact on business.

Communicating the environmental friendliness of a company's goods and services through advertising is a crucial part of green marketing. Ecological, environmentally sustainable, and nature-friendly attractions are examples (Majeed, 2022) that fall within this category. Companies have shifted their tactics to adopt greener methods of conducting business in response to rising consumer interest in environmental protection over the last few decades. Green marketing is expanding and gaining increasing popularity. Advertising on social media has become increasingly important as more consumers use these platforms to research and purchase products. Although studies have examined green marketing and advertising, their presence and impact on social media platforms have largely been overlooked. This research, presented as a systematic review, examines the latest practices and advancements in green social media marketing. Green commercials aim to convey the product's features, costs, and value for the money, as well as the availability and accessibility of the product and related information (Bagdare, 2018). The initiative's overarching goal is to increase consumers' familiarity with and comfort with eco-friendly products.

Eco-labelling

The primary goal of product labeling initiatives is to promote environmentally responsible consumption habits, and the secondary goal is to encourage productive organizations, governments, and other stakeholders to raise environmental standards throughout the economy's product and service supply chain. Eco-labelling is a globally adopted voluntary system for certifying and labeling products based on their environmental performance. Products and services that have been independently verified as being environmentally favorable within a given category earn an "Eco" designation. Consumers and business buyers can quickly and easily discover products that surpass sustainability requirements and are therefore rated "environmentally preferred" due to eco-labels, which are indications placed on product packaging or in e-catalogues. Eco-labels can be owned or administered by a variety of entities, including government departments, nonprofit environmental advocacy groups, and private businesses. Eco-labels can be "single attribute," meaning they only evaluate one aspect of a product's life cycle (the "usage phase") or one environmental issue. They may also be multi-attribute, meaning that they address many environmental concerns (such as energy use, chemical consumption, recycling, and more) that arise over the course of a product's life cycle (production, use, maintenance, disposal). Using information gathered throughout a product's life cycle, eco-labels identify the product(s) with the lowest environmental impact within a specific category. Eco-labelling promotes market-driven environmental improvement by increasing the demand and supply of environmentally friendly goods and services. Eco-labelling accomplishes its three key goals (Verma, 2023): encouraging innovation in the environmental and efficiency sector; engaging consumers; and, most importantly, protecting the environment. Consumers who are more informed about the environmental effects of the products they buy, due to eco-labelling, are more likely to make responsible purchasing decisions. A society that is more cautious and careful in its treatment of the environment as a result of such decisions will emerge over time. Consumers can benefit greatly from eco-labels, making them an essential part of green marketing communication. Eco-labels inform consumers that a product is environmentally safe and that its ingredients are sourced in an ethical and responsible manner. Suki *et al.*(2016) found that consumers' awareness of green marketing increased when they trusted eco-labels and were likely to switch to green products.

Eco-Friendly Packing

Green packaging, also known as sustainable packaging, reduces the environmental impact of product packaging by utilizing energy-efficient packaging processes and materials that are recyclable or biodegradable. Products are displayed for sale to customers in their original packaging. Thus, the packaging serves as a medium for conveying meaning and data through its material components (Underwood, 2003). Despite the ever-increasing variety of products sold in modern supermarkets (Kuvykaite *et al.* 2009), packaging has played a crucial role in conveying information about products throughout their history. Consumers can learn all they need to know about a product without having to bother a salesperson (Meinecke, 1996). Packaging communication stands out due to its persistent influence on sales. This means that the product's communication with the consumer begins at the moment of sale, continues throughout consumption, and typically concludes only when the product has been completely used. Energy is conserved in the production of sustainable packaging, as it is derived from renewable resources, such as paper and cardboard (Merton, 2016). Businesses should think about green packaging as a competitive strategy (Tuwanku *et al.*, 2018). Eco-friendly packaging typically utilizes biodegradable or recycled materials to minimize its environmental impact and reduce the carbon footprint of its production process. Additionally, production processes are becoming increasingly environmentally friendly, utilizing fewer raw materials and having a reduced impact on the planet. Sustainable packaging is adaptable, with a wide range of potential applications across all of the industries that rely heavily on conventional packaging. It is preferable to standard packaging because manufacturers can reuse it multiple times without any loss in value.

Green Corporate Communications

The management of a company's public image can be influenced by effective internal and external corporate communication. Management communication, marketing communication, and business communication are the three main subsets of corporate communication. Effective communication within an organization helps keep everyone aligned, ensuring that tasks are completed efficiently. Externally, corporate communication serves multiple functions, including preserving the company's brand identity, shaping its reputation, handling crises, and resolving confusion about the company's products and services. The main purpose of corporate messaging is to spread a positive image of the organization through various channels of distribution. Corporate communications incorporate additional goals that are essential to a business's success.

Green Website (Eco-friendly Online Platform)

Improved employee morale and retention may result when workers see that their employer cares about both the environment and their well-being. Given the significant amount of time people spend online, it makes sense for businesses to maintain a strong digital presence. Websites and social media profiles have become essential tools for companies of all sizes. Creating and maintaining a green website is one way to reduce the environmental impact of information technology activities. This process not only enhances sustainability but also promotes more efficient practices. Setting green website objectives motivates businesses to develop eco-friendly products and procedures. The public's impression of a company is enhanced when a green website is employed. A growing number of consumers are looking to support environmentally conscious businesses. One of the most important aspects of a website is that clients may use it to access services or obtain the information they need at any time, not just during normal business hours. The website is always active, so customers may place orders from the convenience of their own homes (Ehsan, 2021). One of the most crucial factors to consider when launching a company is its credibility. Having a website designed by a professional web development firm that makes use of cutting-edge web design technologies may do wonders for a company's reputation. Any company would be wise to outsource customer service. In contrast to paying support staff, providing customer service online is simpler and cheaper. It is recommended that dedicated websites be created detailing the origins and manufacturers of eco-friendly goods.

Social Media

Internet-based programs and websites comprise "social media," which enables the sharing of user-generated content and fosters relationships between users from diverse backgrounds. The traditional marketer-consumer dynamic has been upended by social media marketing (Al-Zyoud, 2018). Ismail (2017) identified five main objectives for any social media marketing campaign: brand recognition, brand enhancement, customer acquisition, connection building, and awareness.

Compared to print media, which creates considerable favorable intentions, internet communication of green practices promotes relatively more positive attitudes about advertisements, as reported by Chan *et al.*(2006). Therefore, both are required to increase public consciousness. In addition, survey results suggest that respondents from three businesses prefer to be contacted *via* email when learning about and being advertised green products (Awan & Wamiq, 2016).

BENEFITS OF GMC

Reinforce Experiences

The power of communication extends to the reinforcement of experiences. Convincing someone to engage in an exchange can involve drawing their attention to a problem they may be experiencing or highlighting the positive outcomes of similar deals in the past. Additionally, firms can offer comfort or reassurance either before an exchange takes place or, more typically, after a purchase has been completed. This is crucial, as retaining the consumers firms already have is a much more cost-effective strategy for growing the business than continually trying to attract new ones.

Differentiator

Subsequently, communication regarding marketing can serve as a point of differentiation, especially in highly competitive sectors. GMC refers to the marketing and advertising efforts that have helped shape consumers' perceptions of a product's brand. Brands can be differentiated from one another and positioned effectively through targeted advertising strategies, instilling confidence in their products and fostering a positive outlook among consumers. As a result, communication can serve to educate, convince, reinforce, and construct images in order to distinguish products and services (Fill, 2002).

Brand Credibility (Corporate Reputation)

The reliability of a brand is measured by how faithfully customers perceive their purchases to have met their expectations. Trust in a brand comes from knowing that people will receive what they promise. Products should deliver exactly what they promise in advertising. Having accomplished this, consumers will have more faith in the brand. To keep the company's objectives at the forefront of employees' minds, the corporate communication department may employ promotional materials, crisis communication strategies, and other tactics.

Brand Talent

The employees determine the company's level of success. Training, team meetings, memorandums, and other forms of internal communication can all contribute to the development of the brand's human resources. However, the content and events a firm hosts must be worthwhile and not merely a formality if the firm wants to retain the top talent it has lured to its organization.

Competitive Edge

Companies can gain a competitive edge through improved communications if they improve the quality of their messages. The importance of this is shown in the message's regularity, timeliness, volume, and tone. When communicating with a specific audience, a promotional program is created and implemented when barriers to positive consumer behavior exist, such as strong competition or a lack of motivation or conviction.

Brand Awareness/Corporate Identity

Reputation management is the process of creating recognizable brand names for a firm in the minds of consumers and employees. Branding establishes the public's perception of a corporation and its products. Corporate communication departments are responsible for shaping and promoting positive internal and external perceptions of the company's brand. The value of a memorable name associated with a well-established brand is more than one may expect.

Staff Participation

Top-down employee involvement is crucial for any business. Due to their extensive social networks, employees are well-positioned to communicate with potential customers on behalf of the company. It is crucial to provide workers with the resources they need to share, as this can have a direct impact on the company's bottom line.

Possibility of Penetrating Untapped Markets

Green marketing communication enables firms to expand into new markets. Businesses that want to produce and sell green products must modify their manufacturing processes, switch to more sustainable materials, and utilize recyclable or compostable packaging. The market for environmentally friendly products is still in its infancy. Firms can enter a new market by emphasizing environmental consciousness in their marketing efforts.

A Means of Exchange Itself

The benefits of communications are often intangible, such as the enjoyment one derives from viewing a television commercial or interacting with a brand on social media. Communications can also be viewed as a vehicle for disseminating and spreading a community's shared beliefs and norms.

Workers Productivity

Higher workforce productivity leads to increased revenue and reduced operational costs. This is achievable, provided that employees communicate accurately and do not mislead customers, colleagues, or themselves. When important company news needs to be shared, strategic corporate communications teams are skilled at identifying the right people to deliver the message effectively.

CASE STUDIES: SUCCESSES AND FAILURES IN GREEN MARKETING

Real-world case studies provide valuable insights into the effectiveness and challenges of green marketing strategies. By examining both successful and unsuccessful initiatives, businesses can gain a deeper understanding of the practical implications of environmental messaging and the importance of authenticity in green marketing.

One notable success story is Patagonia's "Do not Buy This Jacket" campaign, launched during the Black Friday shopping season. In a bold move, the outdoor apparel company urged its customers to reconsider unnecessary purchases and reflect on the environmental impact of their consumption. Rather than harming sales, this campaign enhanced Patagonia's credibility and commitment to sustainability, strengthening customer loyalty and ultimately boosting revenue (Fishman, 2015). The campaign exemplified how a brand can build trust and value by aligning its marketing with genuine environmental ethics.

Conversely, the Target "Clean" label controversy illustrates the pitfalls of greenwashing, where companies exaggerate or misrepresent their environmental credentials. Target introduced the "Target Clean" label to signify products free from harmful ingredients. However, critics and legal complaints revealed that some labeled products still contained chemicals considered unsafe, raising questions about the transparency and criteria of the labeling system (Browning, 2021). This backlash damaged consumer trust and highlighted the reputational and legal risks companies face when sustainability claims are not backed by rigorous standards.

Another cautionary example is Oatly's misleading green claims. The UK's Advertising Standards Authority banned several of the brand's advertisements for overstating the environmental benefits of its oat-based products. Claims, such as Oatly's products generating significantly fewer greenhouse gas emissions than dairy alternatives, were found to lack sufficient evidence or proper context (BBC News, 2021). This incident underscores the critical need for accuracy, evidence-based claims, and regulatory compliance in green marketing. Misleading messages not only jeopardize brand integrity but can also attract legal scrutiny.

IMPLICATIONS

The research offers important takeaways for both green customers and marketers alike, and it persuasively argues for a new green age. Therefore, it is essential for marketers to continue initiatives aimed at disseminating information about being environmentally friendly. In order to make more eco-friendly data accessible, marketers need to expand their efforts in creating displays, sampling, marketing, and delivery. Businesses can evaluate their current sustainability initiatives and efforts, then develop and implement a suitable marketing and PR campaign. Many advertising and marketing communications firms now have dedicated departments to social and environmental marketing. Bringing in experts with a focus on ecology could help give these initiatives a boost. To put their sustainability communication plans into action, businesses may team up with NGOs or local communities. Businesses should exercise caution when developing their promotional initiatives by avoiding exaggerated or deceptive claims regarding the positive environmental effects. Recognizing their role in environmentally friendly growth and supporting it through environmentally conscious marketing tactics can be extremely beneficial for businesses. Writing, presenting, statistical analysis, analytical abilities, and technical savvy are just a few of the numerous options necessary for success in the field of company interactions, both at the executive and professional levels. The success of any business would be impossible without its efforts. Businesses that produce and sell goods should promote the environmentally friendly features of their products, especially when those features contribute to overall sustainability. This research sheds light on the current state of green advertising studies, as well as their potential for expansion and development. In light of rising consumer concerns about sustainability, this research will enable the industry to gain new insights into the expanding field of green marketing, which can be applied in their marketing efforts. Creating dedicated online resources that detail the origins and manufacturers of eco-friendly products helps build transparency and trust. Promoting these products through social media platforms like Facebook and Instagram enables two-way communication between companies and consumers, fostering engagement and feedback.

CONCLUSION

As a part of the marketing mix, promotion disseminates the marketing proposition to potential customers. It is the responsibility of a well-planned and integrated set of communication activities to effectively communicate with each of an organization's stakeholder groups. However, there is implicit and important communication through the other elements of the marketing mix (such as a high price, which is often symbolic of high quality). Corporate communications, sustainability disclosure, public relations, CSR, product advertising, product display and demonstration, eco-labeling, and packaging are all important parts of green marketing communication. Therefore, GMC is defined in this chapter as a management process by which an organization sustainably interacts with its multiple target audiences. Organizations create and disseminate messages to their designated stakeholder groups by first learning where and how they are most likely to receive them. Audiences are prompted to provide cognitive, affective, and behavioral responses when messages of great value are communicated. Eco-labeling should consider more than just the reduction of harmful chemicals. It should also account for: 1) the use of renewable, recycled, and sustainably sourced materials; 2) the reduction of embodied energy and greenhouse gas emissions during production; and 3) the improvement of the product's environmental performance throughout its lifecycle.

REFERENCES

Al-Zyoud, M.F. (2018). Social media marketing, functional branding strategy and intentional branding. *Problems and Perspectives in Management, 16*(3), 102-116.
[http://dx.doi.org/10.21511/ppm.16(3).2018.09]

Ankit and Mayur (2013). Green Marketing: Impact of Green Advertising on Consumer Purchase Intention. *Advances Manage,* 6(9), 14-17.

Awan, A.G., Wamiq, S. (2016). Relationship between environmental awareness and green marketing. *Sci. Int. (Lahore), 28*(3), 2959.

Bagdare, S. (2018). Marketing Communications for Sustainable Consumption: A Conceptual Framework. *International Journal of Marketing and Business Communication, 7*(4), 45-49. http://publishingindia.com/ijmbc/

Biloslavo, R., Trnavčevič, A. (2009). Web sites as tools of communication of a "green" company. *Manage. Decis., 47*(7), 1158-1173.
[http://dx.doi.org/10.1108/00251740910978359]

Chang, C. (2011). Feeling Ambivalent About Going Green. *Journal of Advertising, 40*(4), 19-32.
[http://dx.doi.org/10.2753/JOA0091-3367400402]

Chan, R.Y.K., Leung, T.K.P., Wong, Y.H. (2006). The effectiveness of environmental claims for services advertising. *Journal of Services Marketing, 20*(4), 233-250.
[http://dx.doi.org/10.1108/08876040610674580]

Cheema, A. K. H, & Shankar, F. S. (2011). Role of knowledge management to bring innovation: an integrated approach. *Cell., 92*(333), 6183035.
[http://dx.doi.org/10.1108/08876040610674580]

Ehsan, T. (2021). *Why Website is Important for a Business.*https://www.linkedin.com/pulse/why-websit--important-business-talhah-ehsan

Fan, X., & Zeng, S. (2011). Implementation of green marketing strategy in China: A study of the green food industry. (Master's thesis), University of Gävle, China.

Fill, C. (2002). *Marketing Communications* Financial Times Prentice-Hall.(3rd edn..). Harrow:

Goel, S., & Sharma, R. (2017). Developing a financial inclusion index for India. *Procedia Computer Science*, 122, 949-956.

Ganganaboina, A.Y., Sana, R. (2017). *Communication of Green Marketing Strategies for Creating Consumer Awareness: A Study of Grocery Retail Sector in Sweden.*https://www.diva-portal.org/smash/get/diva2

Genç, R. (2017). The importance of communication in sustainability & sustainable strategies. *Procedia Manuf., 8*, 511-516.
[http://dx.doi.org/10.1016/j.promfg.2017.02.065]

Ismail, A.R. (2017). The influence of perceived social media marketing activities on brand loyalty. *Asia Pac. J. Mark. Log., 29*(1), 129-144.
[http://dx.doi.org/10.1108/APJML-10-2015-0154]

Ktisti, E., Hatzithomas, L., Boutsouki, C. (2022). Green Advertising on Social Media: A Systematic Literature Review. *Sustainability (Basel), 14*(21), 14424.
[http://dx.doi.org/10.3390/su142114424]

Kim, W.H., Malek, K., Roberts, K.R. (2019). The effectiveness of green advertising in the convention industry: an application of a dual coding approach and the norm activation model *Journal of Hospitality and Tourism Management, 39*, 185-192.

Kumar, P., Kumar, P. (2017). Intents of green advertisements. *Asia Pacific Journal of Marketing and Logistics, 29*(1), 70-79.
[http://dx.doi.org/10.1108/APJML-03-2016-0044]

Kuvykaite, R., Dovaliene, A., & Navickiene, L. (2009). Impact of package elements on consumer's purchase decision. Economics and management, (14), 441-447.

Kusuma, E.I., Surya, J., Suhendra, I. (2017). Pengaruh strategi green marketing dan pengetahuan lingkungan terhadap keputusan pembelian melalui minat beli sebagai variabel intervening (studi pada member Tupperware di Kota Rangkasbitung) *J. Ris. Bisnis Manaj. Tirtayasa, 1*, 33-49.

Majeed, M. (2022). Green Marketing Communication and Consumer Response in Emerging Markets. In: Mogaji, E., Adeola, O., Adisa, I., Hinson, R.E., Mukonza, C., Kirgiz, A.C., (Eds.), *Green Marketing in Emerging Economies.*. Cham: Palgrave Studies of Marketing in Emerging Economies. Palgrave Macmillan.
[http://dx.doi.org/10.1007/978-3-030-82572-0_3]

Merton, R. (2016). Manifest and latent functions. In Social theory re-wired (pp. 68-84). Routledge.

Meinecke, M. (1996). Patterns of stylistic changes in Islamic architecture: Local traditions *versus* migrating artists, 2, NYU Press.

Mogaji, E., Adeola, O., Adisa, I., Hinson, R.E., Mukonza, C., Kirgiz, A.C. (2022). Green Marketing in Emerging Economies: Communication and Brand Perspective: An Introduction. In: Mogaji, E., Adeola, O., Adisa, I., Hinson, R.E., Mukonza, C., Kirgiz, A.C., (Eds.), *Green Marketing in Emerging Economies.*. Cham: Palgrave Macmillan.
[http://dx.doi.org/10.1007/978-3-030-82572-0_1]

Mohd Suki, N. (2016). Determinants of consumers' purchase intentions of organic vegetables: Some insights from Malaysia. Journal of food products marketing, 24(4), 392-412.

Puspitasari, C., Yuliati, L., Afendi, F. (2021). Pengaruh green marketing, kesadaran lingkungan, dan kesehatan terhadap keputusan pembelian produk pangan organik melalui sikap *J. Apl. Manaj. Bisnis, 7*(3), 713-722.

[http://dx.doi.org/10.17358/jabm.7.3.713]

Tan, Z., Sadiq, B., Bashir, T., Mahmood, H., Rasool, Y. (2022). Investigating the Impact of Green Marketing Components on Purchase Intention: The Mediating Role of Brand Image and Brand Trust. *Sustainability (Basel), 14*(10), 5939.
[http://dx.doi.org/10.3390/su14105939]

Trivedi, K., Trivedi, P., Goswami, V. (2018). Sustainable marketing strategies: Creating business value by meeting consumer expectation. *Int. J. Manag. Econ. Soc. Sci., 7*(2), 186-205.

Tiwari, S., Tripathi, D.M., Srivastava, U., Yadav, P.K. (2011). Green marketing-emerging dimensions. *J. Bus. Excell., 2*, 18-23.

Auliandri, T.A., Armanu, Rohman, F., & Rofiq, A. (2018). Does green packaging matter as a business strategy? Exploring young consumers' consumption in an emerging market. Problems and Perspectives in Management, 16(2), 376-384.
[http://dx.doi.org/10.21511/ppm.16(2).2018.34]

Stoica, M. (2021). Green Marketing Communication Strategies: An Integrative. The Annals of the University of Oradea. Economic Sciences, 1(1), 388-396.

Suki, N.M., Suki, N.M., Azman, N.S. (2016). Impacts of corporate social responsibility on the links between green marketing awareness and consumer purchase intentions. *Problems and Perspectives in Management, 37*, 262-268.
[http://dx.doi.org/10.1016/S2212-5671(16)30123-X]

Shabbir, M.S., Bait Ali Sulaiman, M.A., Hasan Al-Kumaim, N., Mahmood, A., Abbas, M. (2020). Green Marketing Approaches and Their Impact on Consumer Behavior towards the Environment—A Study from the UAE. *Sustainability (Basel), 12*(21), 8977. [CrossRef].
[http://dx.doi.org/10.3390/su12218977]

Siddique, M.Z.R., Hossain, A. (2018). Sources of Consumers Awareness toward Green Products and Its Impact on Purchasing Decision in Bangladesh. *Journal of Sustainable Development, 11*(3), 9-22.
[http://dx.doi.org/10.5539/jsd.v11n3p9]

Tuwanku, A.A., Rohman, F. and Rofiq, A., (2018). Does green packaging matter as a business strategy? Exploring young consumers' consumption in an emerging market. Problems and Perspectives in Management, 16(2), 376.

Underwood, R. L. (2003). The communicative power of product packaging: creating brand identity *via* lived and mediated experience. Journal of marketing theory and practice, 11(1), 62-76.

Verma, S. (February 15, 2023). Importance Of Ecolabelling: An Overview. https://enterclimate.com/blog/importance-of-ecolabelling-an-overview/.

SUBJECT INDEX

A

Accountability 4, 15, 16, 25, 32, 41, 42, 71
Advertising 2, 4, 24, 31, 47, 54, 85, 87, 88, 89, 94, 96
  Green 2, 4, 31, 54, 85, 88, 89, 94
Affordability 13, 30, 42, 43, 48
AI (Artificial Intelligence) 15, 44, 45
Authenticity 2, 6, 11, 13, 16, 17, 31, 32, 38, 43, 87, 94
Awareness 1, 13, 27, 48, 49, 52, 63, 67, 72, 81, 84, 85, 87, 90, 95

B

Behavior 2, 4, 6, 15, 21, 29, 33, 37, 38, 44, 45, 59, 63, 66, 67, 86, 88, 92
  Consumer 2, 4, 6, 21, 29, 33, 38, 44, 59, 63, 86
Benefits 1, 4, 15, 20, 24, 31, 37, 40, 41, 53, 54, 62, 64, 73, 75, 76, 81, 84, 85, 89, 95, 96
  Environmental 1, 4, 15, 20, 24, 31, 37, 40, 41, 53, 54, 62, 64, 73, 75, 76, 81, 84, 85, 89, 95, 96
  Perceived 64
Biodegradable 3, 5, 30, 45, 51, 72, 73, 75, 76, 79, 81, 82, 90, 93
Biomaterial 73
  Starch-based 73
Blockchain 15, 44, 45
Brand 2, 4, 5, 6, 15, 16, 20, 21, 24, 29, 31, 32, 37, 38, 39, 41, 42, 43, 45, 47, 49, 53, 55, 61, 63, 64, 70, 71, 75, 77, 81, 86, 92, 93, 94, 95
  Equity 2, 6, 29, 37, 45
  Loyalty 4, 29, 31, 38, 42, 45, 55, 94
  Reputation 6, 20, 24, 32, 47, 61, 64, 71, 75, 77, 81
  Sustainable 5, 6, 21, 38, 45

C

Carbon 2, 3, 5, 15, 16, 30, 42, 53, 59, 75, 78, 81, 82, 96
  Accountability 16
  Emissions 3, 15, 16, 30, 42, 53, 59, 75, 81, 82, 96
  Footprint 2, 5, 15, 16, 53, 75, 78, 81
  Labeling 15
Case Studies 13, 14, 15, 30, 42, 77, 80, 81, 94
Certification 2, 5, 6, 11, 17, 31, 32, 37, 39, 41, 43, 49, 52, 61, 64, 71, 77, 82
Challenges 1, 2, 10, 11, 22, 33, 38, 40, 41, 47, 59, 64, 70, 77, 78, 79, 82, 94
Circular Economy 8, 72, 76
Communication 5, 8, 11, 17, 22, 25, 27, 28, 31, 32, 37, 39, 43, 45, 48, 52, 54, 55, 77, 78, 84, 85, 87, 88, 90, 91, 92, 93, 95, 96
  Corporate 84, 85, 90, 91, 93, 96
  Green marketing 84, 85, 87, 88, 89, 90, 92, 93, 95, 96
  Green corporate 90, 91
  Sustainable 25, 87, 92
Competition 3, 5, 6, 10, 29, 37, 41, 42, 45, 48, 49, 59, 63, 64, 67, 77, 85, 86, 92, 93
  Competitive advantage 5, 10, 29, 37, 42, 45, 49, 64, 67, 85, 86, 93
Compostable 30, 72, 73, 76, 79, 90, 93
Consumer 2, 4, 5, 6, 8, 11, 13, 14, 15, 21, 22, 26, 29, 30, 31, 32, 33, 37, 38, 39, 40, 41, 42, 44, 45, 47, 48, 49, 53, 55, 59, 63, 66, 67, 71, 72, 75, 76, 80, 82, 84, 86, 87, 88, 94
  Behavior 2, 4, 6, 21, 29, 33, 38, 44, 59, 63, 86
  Conscious (Eco-conscious) 2, 6, 13, 14, 30, 38, 40, 48, 49, 53, 63, 66, 67, 72, 75, 76, 84, 88
  Engagement 5, 8, 15, 22, 32, 37, 38, 39, 45, 48, 71, 80, 87
  Loyalty 4, 13, 29, 31, 38, 42, 45, 55, 94
  Mindset 63

W

www.ingramcontent.com/pod-product-compliance
Lightning Source LLC
Chambersburg PA
CBHW041447210326
41599CB00004B/160